T0330500

David Taylor's
Inside Track

**Provocative insights into the
world of IT in business**

David Taylor's Inside Track

Provocative insights into the world of IT in business

OXFORD AUCKLAND BOSTON JOHANNESBURG MELBOURNE NEW DELHI

Butterworth-Heinemann
Linacre House, Jordan Hill, Oxford OX2 8DP
225 Wildwood Avenue, Woburn, MA 01801-2041
A division of Reed Educational and Professional Publishing Ltd

A member of the Reed Elsevier plc group
First published 2000
Transferred to digital printing 2004
© David Taylor 2000

British Library Cataloguing in Publication Data
Taylor, David A.
    Inside track: provocative insights into the world of IT in business
    1. Business – Data processing   2. Information technology
    I. Title
    658'.05

ISBN 0 7506 4745 0

Library of Congress Cataloguing in Publication Data
Taylor, David.
    Inside track: provocative insights into the world of IT in business/David Taylor.
    p. cm. – (Butterworth-Heinemann/Computer Weekly Professional series)
    Includes index.
    ISBN 0 7506 4745 0
    1. Information technology – Management.   2. Information resources management.
    I. Title.   II. Computer weekly professional series
    HD30.2 .T39 2000   99-089278
    658.4'038–dc21

Typeset by Avocet Typeset, Brill, Aylesbury, Bucks

Contents

Butterworth-Heinemann/ *Computer Weekly* Professional Series

John Riley, Managing Editor, *Computer Weekly*
David Taylor, CERTUS
Terry White, AIS, Johannesburg

There are few professions which require as much continuous updating as that of the IT executive. Not only does the hardware and software scene change relentlessly, but also ideas about the actual management of the IT function are being continuously modified, updated and changed. Thus keeping abreast of what is going on is really a major task.

The Butterworth Heinemann/*Computer Weekly* Professional Series has been created to assist IT executives keep up-to-date with the management ideas and issues of which they need to be aware.

Aims and objectives

One of the key objectives of the series is to reduce the time it takes for leading edge management ideas to move from the academic and consulting environments into the hands of the IT practitioner. Thus, this series employs appropriate technology to speed up the publishing process. Where appropriate some books are supported by CD-ROM or by additional information or templates located on the publisher's web site (http://www.bh.com).

This series provides IT professionals with an opportunity to build up a bookcase of easily accessible but detailed information on the important issues that they need to be aware of to successfully perform their jobs as they move into the new millennium.

Would you like to be part of this series?

Aspiring or already established authors are invited to get in touch with me if they would like to be published in this series:

Dr Dan Remenyi, Series Editor (Remenyi@compuserve.com)

Series titles

IT investment – Making a business case
Effective measurement and management of IT – Costs and benefits (fourth edition)
Stop IT project failures through risk management
Marketing on the web for IT professionals
Understand the Internet
How to manage the IT help desk
E-commerce and data security
Internet and Intranet development
Prince version 2: A practical handbook
Considering computer contracting?
A hackers guide to project management

Foreword

It is very difficult to be a successful IT executive. The technology is demanding, the business processes to be optimized are complex and the environment in which the IT executive works is a minefield of corporate politics, personal agendas and shifting priorities. Furthermore, the workload of most IT executives is simply punitive.

So what help is there for hard pressed IT executives to learn how to achieve a high level of excellence in their profession. The amount of help available is actually very limited indeed. There is little established IT management theory to guide executives. Generally speaking IT practitioners have their noses so close to the grindstone that they do not come up with much general thinking or guidelines about their profession. Of course, the IT consultants are there but, by and large, they are geared up to help big companies with big projects or solve big problems for big fees. The universities are there too. They offer various degree programmes and sometimes short courses. The knowledge available through this channel is often very specialized.

Fortunately there are some sources for solid practical knowledge about successful IT management and one of these is David Taylor. With some twenty years' experience in the IT profession David has lived through every aspect of IT management. He has seen both the upside potential of IT as well as experienced the difficult challenges that it sometimes has to offer. He has worked in just about every role in the profession, eventually working his way up to the position of IT director in a large public company.

On top of this experience David Taylor is one of the most creative thinkers in the IT profession, which he has demonstrated by his ability to solve a wide range of IT problems for organizations large and small. Time and again David generates good, practical ideas which work. He is, in fact, a passionate powerhouse of ideas about how to make IT management more successful and more professional. And his passion for his profession is contagious.

Today, David Taylor is a leading IT consultant who has also taken on the challenge of leading CERTUS, an important forum through which IT directors can share experiences and thinking. David also exerts influence on government policy related to the IT community.

What is especially pleasing about David Taylor and his work is the fact that he has made his thinking accessible to all members of the IT community through his regular column in *Computer Weekly*. In his column David addresses vital IT management issues in a highly accessible and practical way. This has resulted in him having a substantial following of readers who find his thinking useful and who from time to time inundate him with e-mailed comments.

This book is a compilation of David Taylor's weekly column.

I welcome this book not because it provides a source of grand theory about IT management, but because it does not do this. The book provides good practical insights and advice as to how to think about real IT problems and how to find workable solutions. I believe that David Taylor's IT management thinking has a lot to offer members of our profession.

Dr Dan Remenyi

Introduction

This book brings together the first fifteen months of Inside Track columns written for *Computer Weekly*, in their original format and structure. An index of themes is given in the appendix.

For an industry so young we have too many confusing terms and acronyms. None of this is needed – information technology (IT) can be simply explained and easily understood. *Inside track* aims to cut through the strange language we seem to have mastered, and focus on the business imperative.

When I wrote the first column, in July 1998, I never thought this book would be possible. After all, the aim of each is to have its finger firmly on the pulse of the real issues being faced by IT leaders, departments and companies. This 'here and now' approach would surely limit the shelf life of each. However, looking back through the sixty-four columns, the vast majority apply as much today as the day they were written.

Inside track is, first and foremost, a business book. IT is one of the main reasons companies succeed or fail, and IT directors, leaders and managers – the title does not matter – work hard, under incredible pressure, to add value to their organizations. The contributions they are making to the success of UK plc have been unrecognized for too long. Not only are they working in an environment where the scope, scale and speed of change is growing, but the skill set they need becomes greater all the time.

The dedication, quality and importance of the IT leader is central to the messages and themes in the column. To be successful, and drive their organizations forward into the twenty-first century, they must think business first, take risks, and inspire their people.

The column has prompted much reaction, feedback and comment, which is great news. In particular I welcome debate and disagreement, of which there is too little in IT.

No one has all the answers, and in some ways my column is written as a stalking horse, putting forward ideas that may or may not work in the reader's particular company.

I do this because there is not enough positive action taking place in IT to resolve the problems we face, many of which have been unchanged for years. Ideas, insights and inside track are totally useless unless they lead to positive, powerful action.

In the first year, if each reader has found, and put into practice, just one idea that has helped them and their company to gain or retain a customer, increase their revenue, or motivate one person, then it is has been worthwhile.

Each column appears in its original form, which may be different from the final version that appeared in *Computer Weekly*. In addition all headings in the magazine were written by *Computer Weekly*, this book contains the original titles (for better or worse).

David Taylor

Acknowledgements

This book is dedicated to all IT leaders, departments and people, everywhere.

Also for everyone who has helped in my transition from corporate life to free spirit. Listing them all would take a book in itself. For now, for their advice, support and wisdom I thank, in alphabetical order, Adam Afriyie, Robin Bloor, Adrian Gilpin, Nicola Hunt, Hugh Macken, Bob Mcdowell, Brinley Platts, Dan Remenyi and Brindley Reynaud.

Without *Computer Weekly* this would not have been possible, in particular John Riley, Karl Schneider, Hooman Bassirian and Julia Hoare.

Finally, to my family, Rosalind, Anthony and Olivia. Many of the ideas you are about to read have come from these three wonderful people, with whom I have the honour to share my life.

1 | Beyond belief

Crossing fingers while shaking hands used to mean the agreement was worthless, for customers and suppliers these days it more probably means wishing for luck. If the growing evidence is to be believed, trust in each other is dissolving, along with the wasted time, energy and cost involved. What has gone wrong?

Although *Computer Weekly*'s 'Stiffing' campaign focuses mostly on suppliers, that is not the whole story. Many customers, desperate to resolve a business need, take products and services without knowing exactly what will be delivered – or whether it will bring any real benefit to their organization.

In reality most problems are caused by genuine misunderstandings, it is not in anyone's interest for things to go wrong. In my experience the following specific actions not only reduce risk, but also help develop a trusted, strategic partnership.

Customers:

1 Clearly define what role the supplier or product will play and the business benefit to be gained. Identify a quantified benefit before buying.

2 Do not attempt to screw your supplier into the ground during contract/price negotiations – you will pay for it later.

3 Consider appointing a full time supplier 'manager' whose role is to ensure relationships with all suppliers are working as agreed.

4 Provide an overall standard to live up to, a code of conduct that suppliers must follow. Never openly criticize any supplier – resolve disputes behind closed doors.

5 Reward supplier delivery by recommending them to other customers, giving them free publicity and involving them in decisions. I know of one company who pays early for excellent work.

Suppliers:

1 Clearly define the benefits of the technology or service – the real customer value. Only accept full payment on delivery of these benefits. That will show you mean business, and believe in your own abilities/product.

2 Be honest when things go wrong. Not only will this win you respect, but every crisis is an opportunity to do that bit extra.

3 Do not make your customers too reliant on your product or services. It may seem attractive to 'tie them in' but it usually has the reverse effect of causing resentment. Let your delivery speak for itself.

4 Bring something extra to the table – an idea or innovation for the customer – it may be completely unrelated to the proposed service.

5 Know your prospective customers. Understanding their business will help you win, keep and develop it.

Sadly, trust and handshakes are not enough, and while contracts have their place (locked away out of sight) they are a last resort. When companies have to rely on contract wordings the relationship is, most likely, beyond repair.

Somewhere between the two extremes of litigation and mutual adulation lies the winning balance that not only avoids serious dispute, but also gives the exciting possibilities of ever closer alliance and opportunity for mutual benefit.

At the moment it is out of control. That is costly enough for the companies involved – for our industry reputation, already under enormous threat, it could be disastrous.

2 | What happens after what comes next?

In January 2000 many IT departments are in for the shock of their lives. Assuming the world does not come to an end, (think of all that wasted time and money if it does!), and that we make the Y2K/EMU deadlines, what next? Many are predicting the IT bubble will burst – in my view they are wrong.

Once Y2K is 'fixed' there will be an enormous demand for all those 'minor' projects that have been on hold, there are thousands of working-days effort around the millennium corner. Many business customers can't wait for IT to, at last, do 'proper work' again.

The good news is for contractors and staff. Resource demand will not fall – in fact in many areas it will continue to grow. Remember what we discovered with Y2K – many of the skills we thought we didn't need any more became important again.

The irony here is that successful post-2000 projects may well provide the real business value that has eluded so many IT projects in the past. At this stage there is little chance of defining exactly what 'information age' or 'digital age' really mean for your company – but now is the time to start working with the business to schedule as far ahead as possible, while identifying the skills required.

Some may say that post Y2K projects should not be treated as anything special, and simply planned in the normal way – but they are as unique as the millennium bug itself and merit special attention now.

Will business ever trust IT again after the Y2K fiasco? Did we handle what was, in reality, a monster of our own making? The rebuilding of business/IT relationships must start now if we are to regain trust.

Start by allocating a good Project Manager to identify the scope and definition of post-Y2K projects. Their role should be to:

- Share the situation with business peers and decision-makers.

- Quantify the skills needed in general terms. Are they available now?

- Identify key staff and retain them beyond the payment of Y2K bonuses – they will be crucial.

- Plan training so it is ready to kick-in as soon as required.

- Ensure that all proposed projects have clear business benefits and the process for these being delivered is in place.

- Set a date by which all of the projects for 2000 will be finalized – September 1999 latest.

The post-millennium scenario will offer many opportunities to drive overall business strategy, reinforce alignments with internal customers and make long term investments in staff.

It was the organizations who saw the Y2K coming that are in the driving seat now, it will be the companies that look beyond that who will really help take their business forward. We must not do a 'Y2K' to our projects. To use the excuse that we didn't see it coming may well be one excuse too many.

3 | Another initiative? Oh joy!

What real financial benefits have been delivered by the 'initiatives' so prevalent in business today? From an IT perspective, under ever increasing pressure to justify our spending and very existence, where are the savings, improvements and competitive advantage resulting from the time, energy and money spent?

Take business process reengineering (BPR). Plausible in its aims to improve processes, effectiveness and very way of working, in its implementation many companies forgot about the most important factor – people. That some BPR exercises were simply an excuse for downsizing is a reason many IS departments are now having to rebuild trust.

Continuous improvement (CI) and 'total quality' are rallying calls that have fallen into disrepute and become synonymous with bureaucracy and large manuals. They are also examples of squashing general catch-all standards into an IT environment – in a service environment the language of some standards is unfamiliar and people have trouble relating to it and appreciating its value. It can take a year to get something 'right first time.' It is better to take action, try things out and get something 80 per cent right. Also, the starting premise that IS departments exist to try to get things wrong is inconceivable.

Properly focused to address key issues and with clear benefits, initiatives have an important role, indeed releasing and applying innovation and creativity will be a major determinant of future success. There are common traits for success:

- Ideas that come from within can be of far greater value than those imposed from outside. Create a culture where ideas can be freely expressed without blame or ridicule (not easy).

- Focus on addressing the big issues such as delivery, staff morale and retention, etc. – don't get bogged down in the drink machine location trivia.

- Beware company and industry initiatives that try to be all things to all people – it is how it will work in *your* department that counts.

- There are ways of reducing numbers or instigating perceived negative change without hiding behind some false premise. People are not stupid.

- Ensure people are empowered to put ideas into action without having to refer them to numerous committees – set priorities quickly.

- Reward innovation and ideas through recognition and monetary payments.

- Emphasize the positive – growth and moving forward – not hunting out mistakes or penny pinching.

- Invest in training and developing people so they do their jobs better.

- Company-wide initiatives should be subject to the same cost versus benefit analysis as other projects and not just pushed to the top of the priority list by default.

Next time such an initiative hits your company or department, ensure it is prioritized and treated like all other project requests. Ask the same basic business questions that accompany any strategic request. What are the costs, timescales and benefits? If there are more questions and uncertainty than answers and direction ask the initiative's sponsor 'why?' If the response is 'why not?' then start clearing some space on your shelves.

4 | Beware of suspect packages

Far from being the panacea that customers hoped and vendors promised, Software packages are often not delivering. As an alternative to developing in-house systems, acquiring a package has always been seen as the simple and inexpensive answer, so why do so many installations go wrong?

Strange as it may seem, customers rarely know what they are buying – failing to look beyond the hype and expectations raised by the supplier. This, coupled with unclear business benefits, leads to inevitable problems.

The amount of work involved in altering the software, or changing business processes to meet the way the package works, is often underestimated. Some of the most spectacular failures have been when tried and tested solutions have been modified. The Stock Exchange's Taurus system, which lost £250 million, was based on a successful package from the USA.

Packages are by definition all things to all buyers, and as business complexity grows few are meeting all of a customer's requirements. This leads to modifications that result in a costly and only partially successful application, and companies end up paying more over a longer period of time than if they had developed a solution in house.

This is a complex subject, but the following covers the main questions to ask:

1 What is my business need, to what extent will the package fit? (Below 75 per cent spells danger).

2 What are the exact deliverables, in what time and to what cost? (Ensure these are in the contract – preferably fixed time with penalties and incentives).

3 Will it work? What is its track record and customer base? How have other customers altered it? (Ask other customers that have used the same version as you are buying, and get guarantees on performance from the supplier).

4 How much will it cost? What is the cost base? (Ensure ongoing maintenance and upgrade costs are known in advance, numbers of users are agreed and whether subsidiary companies can use the software).

5 Is it documented? How much education, training and consultancy are included within the basic cost of the software?

6 Who owns the title to the software? Is a parent company or third party involved? (Make sure you have an Escrow agreement in place – such an agreement allows for provision of the source code to be passed to customers in the event of the supplier ceasing to trade).

7 What is the source code written in? Is it in line with my strategy and skills base? (Don't become too reliant on the supplier for advice or skills).

8 How do we get changes made to the package after it goes live? Is there a user group? (User groups are useful for experience sharing but you may have to convince them that your need is a priority).

All of this said, a package can indeed be the best and most economic solution, providing everyone is clear what it can and cannot do. Know what you are buying and only buy a package if you can install it with the absolute minimum of changes. Don't let this philosophy be hijacked – tampering with suspect packages can be very dangerous.

5 | Our ultimate challenge

If our industry has tears, it should prepare to shed them now. We knew that people retention and skill shortages were a growing problem – few could have predicted the devastating effect it would have on business strategy, the economy and our country.

Computer Weekly's Banner Research survey has revealed that over one in five organizations has had to change its IT strategy to match available skills. We are in a situation where the skills of our people are determining what we can achieve and the projects we can deliver like boarding a ship for Calais and ending up in the Isle of Wight because the captain couldn't read the charts. This is a crisis, which calls for leadership, focus and action.

I suppose we should have seen it coming, and in many ways we are simply reaping what we have sown in the past when we neglected to invest in our people. It is easy to blame the head-hunters and contract markets – but that is not the whole story – the 1980s' fad for business process re-engineering destroyed morale and trust.

Any IT director not working on staff retention is risking the whole future of their department.

Staff turnover can be reduced – it has been done in several organizations. By investing in people's development and transforming departments to establish a want to work attitude. By outsourcing the 'noise' on a selective basis and focusing permanent staff on strategic, new technology projects.

Establish a learning culture where people's value is based on their willingness and ability to learn new skills and take on new challenges rather than on being the sole custodian of one or two key pieces of information. Share the position with your business customers, do the unusual to tie your staff in, and above all never give up.

As an industry we need to revisit, sanitize and make professional the whole staff procurement process. We must also look hard at our education priorities and funding, at bringing more people in from outside the industry, and in attracting skills from outside the UK, as other countries are actively doing.

If we allow our future business growth to be constrained by the availability of IT skills we will once again be blamed for the fact that business cannot do what it wants and needs to do. Investment in IT will be seen as a waste of money.

It is no good blaming 'circumstances' or events outside of our control – our future, whether IT becomes a major enabler of positive change or drifts into being little more than a necessary evil, is up to all of us.

It is time to restore pride in our industry and our people, to liberate their aspirations and potential, and to lead them towards a compelling destiny.

Our industry is at its lowest point yet – we must all play a part in restoring our business, economic and strategic role. This is the ultimate challenge for our industry; it is up to all of us to rise to that challenge – what are you, personally, going to do?

6 | This is personal

Deborah Graham, 33, a computer systems manager from Dudley, committed suicide after struggling in private to cope with her job. What a tragedy for someone so young to be consumed by such stress, pressures and worries.

These are not unique symptoms, indeed a CW/Banner research shows that over 30 per cent of IS directors feel that stress affects their ability to cope with their job.

IS directors and departments experience levels of demand, deadlines and project deliveries that make our service at least on a par with the traditional pressure areas of sales and marketing.

In many ways we are still treated as servants reacting to our master's needs. Add the ongoing budget restrictions, recent downsizing and the specific pressures of Y2K and staff retention, and it is no surprise that we have reached this position. Other reasons cited to me recently are:

- Working long hours in some companies is still considered 'macho'.

- The growing volume of information we are required to handle.

- Lack of trust in other people to make decisions.

- The 'blame culture' prevalent in many companies – IS managers are easy to blame as they are perceived as being at the end of the corporate chain.

One IS director told me the role of an IS director is to 'take the blame, say sorry and try to keep smiling!'

Companies are in many ways making IS managers scapegoats for business failings by denying them access to timely business intelligence, and then blaming them for not responding appropriately. There are no easy answers to this, however the following will help:

- Work to improve business/IS relationships at all levels, while ensuring your business customers take ownership of projects, priorities and delivery. Market the IS service and the value you bring to your company.

- IS service is a balance between what a company wants and what a company can afford – have clear service charters in place and build in time for proactive activities.

- Investing in prevention is less stressful than spending on cure.

- Outsource the noise on a modular basis – hand over the pressure to specialists without losing control – focus internal staff on strategic projects.

- Put in place an internal mentoring scheme. Also, seek an external mentor for IS managers, who will provide both advice and be a welcome release valve.

- Beware e-mail – it comes across as unfriendly. Maintain personal contact and when you do send e-mails make them friendly and constructive.

- Address culture so that blame is eliminated and there is a community atmosphere where people work for each other.

- Reduce information overload – IS managers do not need to know everything! Go for summaries on key priorities.

There are also many ways to reduce the effects of stress, such as keeping our lives in balance, physically fitness and making time to relax. If you are suffering do take professional advice.

Stress has been an issue in all walks of life for many years. There are, however, a growing number of developments within IT that make it an urgent issue to be addressed, on an industry, corporate and personal basis.

7 Emotions must give way to reason

Staff retention may be the most prominent issue facing IS directors, but supplier relationships are often the most emotive. Trusted partnerships may be the ultimate aim, many would settle for half-decent understanding and fair play.

It is not just the suppliers who must work to improve this, and while *Computer Weekly*'s 'stiffing' campaign has brought the subject to the forefront – the term 'stiffing' is unfortunate, negative and, in itself, divisive.

That said, there are no wrong answers with this subject, the only thing that is wrong is not discussing the question.

Supplier/customer disputes have been quietly destroying time, energy and budgets for many years. *Computer Weekly*, in association with law firm Hammond Suddards, have developed the Software Licence Code.

In many ways the strongest recommendation is the final one on disputes, where the Code advocates an independent arbiter, something that has long been needed. Perhaps a good analogy here is with the employment/trade union fallout of the seventies, when ACAS came to the fore. This is a good idea and should be taken on board. These are the main points of the agreement:

- Plain English. Yes, but a crystal mark is no substitute for talking with existing customers of the software/services.

- Location restrictions. This is a sweeping paragraph that could cost many suppliers dearly – can any one company, for example, simply export their software all over Europe at no extra cost?

- User restrictions. Suppliers have had justifiable complaints for some time over the definition and policing of 'concurrent users,' so if there are to be procedures on named users, there must also be tighter restrictions on concurrent ones.

- Pricing in general. Everyone has to be absolutely clear, up front, what will be paid, when, and for what.

- The outsourcing clause needs to be rewritten in plain English, defining 'serious infringement.' As does the disposals paragraph.

- Integration work also causes problems and would need clarification on a local basis.

My general comments are that the guidelines lean too heavily in favour of the customer. This is not in anyone's interest, least of all the IS departments. There is a need to redress the balance back towards the customer, but going too far will further alienate the relationships. For example, any guidelines must surely include advice on definition of customer requirements, so everyone knows where they stand.

However, all credit to *Computer Weekly* for launching the debate with such a detailed proposal. Many IT associations are already involved.

Let this code be the start of a national IT debate that may start with platitudes, but must result in a new climate of trust and best practice that is driven by IS departments and suppliers, and not by expensive redress to contracts, solicitors and the law.

8 | A date too far?

Thank you, Microsoft. Just as many IS directors have moved to an NT strategy, training their staff accordingly and knowing where they stand on planning, investment and timescales, NT5 is delayed.

That said, how many IS directors really expected NT5 to arrive on time? It is not as if this news is a bolt out of the blue, a delay has been anticipated. Perhaps better to wait for bug-free versions than using used as beta-testers, as has happened in the past.

However, with ongoing training, rising total costs of ownership (TCO) and the need to focus on other things next year, this announcement will cause problems.

As we try to hold together our strategies, in the face of uncertainties ahead in so many other areas, this event cannot be dismissed as just another 'supplier' failing to deliver. We are all too reliant on Microsoft for that.

In many ways we have reached the stage when our very technology strategies, now running only one or two years ahead, depend almost totally on our suppliers' dates and service.

For those who haven't made the NT/NetWare choice, this may indeed tip the balance against Microsoft. Where people are already committed to NT, however, it is a time for keeping our nerve and showing that we can rise to situations like this and meet them as opportunities not disasters. Are we truly only as good as the people who supply us? IT leaders need to respond to this by:

- Reviewing their exposure in terms of projects and business requirements.

- Producing interim strategies that safeguard existing investment.

- Fully brief their people to ensure buy-in.

- Being clear on TCO costs and any budget implications.

- Still making strategic decisions based on business needs

- Putting pressure on Microsoft to emulate the Tom Peter's doctrine, under-promise and over-deliver, or at least come close to it.

The implication that this is a good reason for switching from Microsoft to Novell, is not fully justified as the switch in skill sets could cost considerably more than any delays which might be incurred. In any case we should base our strategy on what is best for the job and not what is available. The fact is, it's a delay not a cancellation, and it may well be that when it does arrive NT will emerge as the product that we have long hoped for.

Many will seize this opportunity to attack Microsoft, others will use it as an excuse for not delivering. The real heroes will be those who are able to meet the needs of their companies in the face of this additional challenge.

I well remember 23 August 1995, and the midnight queues ahead of the first release of Windows 95. One of the reasons for Microsoft's dominance is their ability to hit the market at exactly the right time with exactly the right product.

Most IS directors, that I know, were ready for NT5 when it was promised. How long will the queues be, next year?

9 | If we are to attract the right people, we need to improve our looks

Staff shortages are a long-term problem that need long-term solutions, one of which is the recruitment and training of people from non-IT backgrounds.

A recent Apex survey (*Computer Weekly*, 27 August 1998) showed three-quarters of students are so unimpressed with IT that they are unwilling to consider it as a career. These are disturbing findings, especially with the high PC usage, and general awareness, among this age group.

- We have to overcome this by ensuring that IT becomes a 'brand' industry and career path in its own right.

- We need closer links between academic learning and corporate IT skills – perhaps a best practice for IT education.

Our image does not help recruit those with some working experience, either. To many, it seems that learning IT is like learning a musical instrument – you either do it when you are young or not at all. This is nonsense, of course, and there are many examples to prove that people at any age can change to a career in IT once the unnecessary mystique has been removed.

It is crazy that while IT departments need long-term resourcing, there are many good business people that want to learn IT skills. Given this climate it is hardly surprising that some training companies are charging exorbitant sums for teaching people.

- We must manage people's expectations in what can be realistically learned over what period. Companies could offer apprenticeships linked to specific skill development – involving contractors and suppliers in cross-skilling.

- People working in companies, but outside of the IS function, can be encouraged to join the department and make a change of career.

- IT is the business and the business is IT – there may be opportunities to learn without changing departments.

- Consider secondments across the company – with clear roles and promises in place both for the duration and at the end

There is a skill gap to be addressed and this should be done in two ways – correctively and preventatively. Correctively means the positive encouragement by everyone, Government included, of people re-skilling into IT. Preventatively means the positive encouragement of people choosing an IT career straight from school or college.

There is no doubt that the future of the nation is inextricably linked to our ability to rise to the IT challenge, with the right people, in the right place, with the right skills, at the right time.

It should not be left to individual opportunists to attempt to crack this problem commercially, it has to be a joint effort across IT and society to create a climate where people see a career in IT as a positive move and the industry undertakes to 'look after the valuables'.

This is the only way to break the doom and gloom scenario of turnover, headhunting and skill shortages. Otherwise we will still be facing these major issues in five years time, and we will have learned nothing.

10 | Trading places

Retail success used to depend on location, not any more. The web revolution has changed all that, and all middle companies, resellers and 'agents' should watch out. The very technology – driven by techies, used by nerds and operated in isolation – is changing our lives, and the way we do business, forever.

Now, everywhere is as close as everywhere else. It saves time, money and provides greater choice. Significantly, many now say it offers better customer service, being open twenty-four hours a day.

The net has until now been about communication and information. Now it is about opportunity – and who moves with greatest speed. Amazon.com, the world's biggest bookstore, and Tesco, who now have more loyalty cardholders than some banks have accounts, are two of the most often cited examples.

The main hurdle is security. An important issue, but it will be overcome in the same way it was for telephone shopping and banking.

What, then, does this mean for the internal IS department? Electronic commerce is a golden opportunity for internal IS leaders and their people. With more companies choosing to re-direct their customers from the high street to the net IT in general is finally moving from the back room to the shop window.

Effective web sites and point of sale facilities require a hitherto unprecedented level of cooperation across an organization as technology, product and window dressing combine. In one fell swoop the arguments about IT being separate from business strategy, out of business alignment and ripe for total outsourcing disappear.

What an opportunity to invest in our internal people. By outsourcing the 'noise' on a modular basis, IS departments can focus on the 'music' – activities central to their corporate aim, involvement at the heart of their business. There will be an additional strain on resources and training will be needed. The outcome will be more than worth it – with improved focus, morale and productivity.

There are also many internal implications brought on by internet technology. Many are now predicting the twilight years for the PC, as business find their needs better met by reliable, easy to use devices linked to cheap, corporate-wide processing power.

Recent research from the EIS-Network (1 September 1998) suggests the real issue is not e-commerce, but digital convergence, and corporate alliances. By the time we are completely digital, say 2010, changes will happen that cannot be imagined today. In communications, commerce and all aspects of our lives. Will video conferencing threaten the airline industry? Will everything be a commodity? Will pollution fall as people can work from anywhere and travel less?

The internet itself has been around for more than a quarter of a century; quietly doubling in size while no one was looking. Four years ago, still doubling, it suddenly burst into view. It is the new dial tone and will dictate communications and commerce in the future.

This is an outstanding opportunity for IS to drive business forward, be at the heart of an organization and to be seen as the champion of achievement.

11 | Shall we dance?

Next year's diaries are printed, the year-end parties planned; yet many companies are still not prepared. The message to these organizations is simple – act now and act fast.

Amid the depressing stories of inaction, apparent lack of awareness and deadlines slipping into the impossible, one Y2K story shone through last week. Shell and BP are to review their business partners, suppliers and supply chains to ensure compliance in every company on whom they depend. Some may see this as a 'big brother' audit – it is not. This is a sound business decision, which will deliver benefits all round. Other companies should follow suit.

This is positive, not so much for the obvious health checks, but for the alliances such actions can forge. The successful companies of the next millennium will be those who seek competitive advantage through partnership and synergy. An alliance forged in difficult times could lay the foundations for greater cooperation and mutual benefit.

If such an approach can be taken as a remedial activity now, imagine the positive possibilities for the future. These giant oil players are about to learn a great deal about their suppliers. It is a level of contact that would probably not have happened if it were not for the Y2K problem. Small mercies – huge potential.

All those processes your suppliers have that you don't like, or those restrictions that you put in place that block smooth operations, can now be reviewed, and positive changes made.

Similarly, solutions to the Y2K problem can, and should, be shared. Most companies are paying consultants and contractors to fix Y2K problems only to have the same people move on to another organization and repeat the process all over again.

Action 2000 and other groups have been set up for the right reasons – to pool knowledge, resource and expertise. The rip-off merchants are preying on people's fears and we can only reduce their damage by joining together as a customer community. Even traditional competitors (such as Shell and BP) are now seeing the value of collaboration to address this problem.

It is time for action – and cooperation:

- Identify all suppliers and supply chains.

- Prioritze the risk for each one.

- If you haven't started talking – do so now – right now.

- Set up joint project teams.

- Share knowledge and expertise – there is no point in being the only one with the answer.

- Be willing to share information beyond the immediate issue.

- Map the chain – dependencies and dependants.

- Appoint someone with overall responsibility if you haven't already done so.

- Share and pool resources.

- Have contingency plans in place – prepare for the inevitable casualties and have alternative suppliers lined up.

If ever there was an opportunity to make this a community problem rather than 'every man for himself', then now is the time. There are no more ivory towers, we live in an interdependent world and must 'link hands' against this common enemy.

12 | Supplier fallout

Two professions often accused of inventing their own, mysterious language are lawyers and IT managers. When these two meet, in suppler contracts, many trees die and there is much confusion. In reality contracts are only needed as a last resort, and by that stage much time, energy and money will have been wasted along the way.

Contracts are useful for clarifying roles and deliverables, but they are no substitute for partnership, trust and common goals. They are also not as important as managing a supplier relationship, and service, in a businesslike and professional manner.

Like a marriage, these relationships have to be worked on all the time.

What can IS departments do when things start to go wrong? Misunderstandings or breakdowns in communication cause the vast majority of times when IS/supplier relationships break down. It is rare for a supplier to set out with the aim of ripping-off an IS department.

The relationship should be built on openness and effective communication, and early warning signs should be heeded, and given time and attention. These are the main ones to watch for:

- Failure of either party to attend progress meetings on a regular, or as agreed, basis.

- The need for formal meetings for any minor change to agreements.

- Failure of the supplier to inform the customer of organizational changes which may have an effect on service.

- Niggling problems being raised to an inappropriate level, e.g. IS director.

- Internal IS department's staff regularly blaming a supplier.

- Calls not returned, promises broken, delays with no reason.

- Customers or suppliers throwing their weight around.

- An inappropriate level of focus on cost.

When it does go wrong, there is a tendency for each party to blame the other. Communication, understanding and an objective view are nowhere to be seen. When such relationships do start to go wrong an IS department should:

- Be objective, there are always two sides to a story.

- Be part of the solution – not part of the problem.

- Agree an objective to achieve – not necessarily complete resolution, it may be a milestone along the way.

- Ensure clear ownership on both sides.

- Sit down and talk about it – listen to each other.

- Don't make threats – particularly empty ones.

- Refer to facts and experience, not hearsay and rumour.

- Don't quote the contract unless it clarifies understanding.

- Don't hide behind the 'the customer is always right' chestnut, no one believes it anyway!

If all else fails suggest mediation with an independent third party, the results binding on both customer and supplier.

This is a very hot issue at the moment for IS directors and departments. Successful supplier relationships depend more on people, attitude and communications than on any contract.

If events do deteriorate, contracts and legal action may come into play. However, if you are considering this step, be aware of the cost and consequences, and that it is one step beyond the point of no return.

13 | Bad timing?

IT people work long, unsociable and unpredictable hours, and this often leads to fatigue, stress and counter-productive results. From midnight on 1 October, those total hours must not exceed forty-eight hours per week for each person – unless by personal choice.

This is the main recommendation of the European directive on working hours. What does this mean for IS departments? Is it simply a hammer to crack a nut, or, more disturbingly, to crack a mountain?

The legislation's aim is to be applauded. Long hours worked over many weeks, often in front of a screen in crisis mode, does little for the health of an individual or an organization.

However, the legislation is vague and full of uncertainties. Does it include out of hour's call-out, for example, in response to a disaster? The directive also dictates that no one must work more than six days per week, but does this override the hours per week? It is confusing, does not address the real issues, and gives the impression of simply bringing the UK into line with the rest of Europe.

Too many companies still practice the 'I can stay later than you' ethos, and by requiring employees to sign a waiver to work more hours these companies can now add the 'have you signed up as a loyal employee?' syndrome.

One consequence is certain; there will be an increase in industrial tribunals, which will please the legal profession. Costs may also increase, with contractors increasing their rates to waive their rights under the new directive, and the need to have more people on out of hour's call.

There are wider and more strategic issues here, many of them offering an opportunity to achieve what this legislation does not – improvement in service, clarity and well being.

IT departments that do not have clear contracts with their business customers now need to do so as a matter of urgency. The provision of effective IT service is always a balance between what a company wants and what it can afford, and service charters or service level agreements document that. They also increase ownership and business acumen within IS departments, as well as clarifying responsibilities across the whole organization.

Prevention must now take on a higher importance. Easy to say, more difficult to achieve. The investment needed is difficult to secure with so much focus on time critical projects such as the Y2K and EMU.

The bad news for 'senior' IS managers is that the legislation does not apply to them. They must continue to work whatever hours are needed. Considering that few companies pay overtime at this level, and take little account of work done at home, this legislation fails IS leaders almost completely.

Overall, despite its aims, this legislation will have little direct effect on IT people's well being, morale and potential. However, if it proves a catalyst for addressing the wider human, service and cultural issues, then in the medium to long term it may prove worth the not inconsiderable paper it is written on.

14 | IT directors planning for recession

Is there a recession coming? If there is, what will it mean for IT, its role and impact within organizations, and for IS directors and departments?

It is all very confusing. We hear the doom and gloom scenarios on the news in the morning, and then come into work to face skill shortages, strategic 'must-do' projects such as Y2K and EMU, and growing pressure from business customers.

When recessions hit, it is the non-essential areas that suffer. In the past this has included IT. Not any more. Any recession in 1998 or 1999 will be very different from the early 1990s.

Companies that slash IT spending will be making a very big mistake. Access to information is survival critical to organizations in difficult times, as is the effective deployment of, and investment in, emerging technologies. It is up to the IS director to convince their CEO, and board, that IT is absolutely essential. To do this IT and business strategies must be closely, and inseparably, aligned.

Given that the cycles of boom and bust are inevitable, albeit with different timeframes, contexts and consequences are there any lessons to be learned from the past? The biggest is people, and how they were treated last time round. Much of the panic and downsizing of the early 1990s is behind the crippling and expensive staff shortages faced today.

Recessions do give IS directors an opportunity to ensure their business customers take responsibility and ownership:

- IT projects (including Y2K and EMU) are business projects, and need clear business ownership.

- Now is the time to set clear project priorities.

- Every project must be rigorously assessed to ensure that estimates are as good as they can be. This must include the whole project cycle, including business-testing, etc.

Now is the time, above all, to invest in people. A reduction in projects is an opportunity to restore the balance between full-time staff and contractors. It is a time to clarify what skills should be kept and trained in-house, and what to outsource on a modular basis.

IT leaders must not make drastic reductions across the board, because recessions and booms have one thing in common – they come to an end. When the recession is over we need to be in a position to pick up where we left off, so don't pawn the family silver in pursuit of short-term solvency.

When recessions hit there are no easy answers, which is usually why financial survival takes absolute priority. Now is the chance for IT, and the IS director, to play an active role in shaping the future of their company. CEOs and the board will be looking for direction and answers – IS directors are in a powerful position to gather together the facts and the compelling arguments, and to provide those very answers.

It will be the companies that have IT at their very heart that will see the greatest medium- to long-term competitive benefit, and advantage.

15 | We are not alone!

Working in IT can be a lonely experience, and at times it is easy to believe that the problems and challenges we face are unique to our departments and companies. Combine this belief with some of our realities – internal project demands and budgetary pressures, external skill shortages and threats of recession – and it is no wonder that stress is becoming such a major issue among IT managers and directors.

The good news, if one can call it that, is that the same issues are affecting almost everyone. The whole corporate IT industry is affected, to a greater or lesser degree, by staff shortages, Y2K, EMU, project management and priorities, total cost of ownership and customer/supplier disputes, etc.

Of even greater significance is the perception of internal IS departments, a crucial factor in determining their success. Such perception and attitudes are now determined as much from the overall image and profile of the IT industry, as from any internal actions and policy.

CEOs need strategic answers, and their impressions of our effectiveness will be tarnished by the high-profile project disasters, vendor disputes and overall meaningless terminology and gobbledegook that has infected our industry.

So much for today's reality. With technology changing faster than ever, we need access to the information that will help us make the right decisions, move forward and compete. Finding such data is not easy, and the search itself often leads to information overload.

No IT director is alone. No IT department works in a vacuum. All

IT directors need information, answers and friends. There are specific ways of achieving this:

- Form a strategic alliance with a company of a similar size to yourselves – perhaps in a different industry sector – to meet, compare progress and share problems and solutions.

- Make sure that you, as IT director, are your CEO's main source of information on IT issues. Encourage your CEO and business managers to attend external business/IT events – and go with them.

- Form strategic partnerships with your suppliers to keep track of the real information you need.

- Subscribe to a research organization.

- Join with other directors and managers in one of the organizations furthering the interests of corporate IT.

Organizations are more networked now than they have ever been before, both in the technical and human sense. People are more aware of their dependence on others for tangible support in almost all aspects of work and personal life.

The IT director in today's world is just as dependent on the activities and tacit support of other IT directors as on their own suppliers or business. It is no longer acceptable to lock themselves away and pull up the drawbridge – more answers probably lie outside than within.

IT is now a global business issue, core to the survival, growth and future of all organizations. It must be high on strategic agendas, and in the minds of every CEO. By transforming our overall profile, perception and positive influence, we can help internal IT departments establish themselves where they belong – at the very heart of an organization.

16 | Design your destiny

No one seems to agree on the biggest issue faced by IT directors today – there are so many to choose from – skills crises, Y2K, EMU, recession, supplier relationships, etc. However, if response to this column is anything to go by, everyone agrees on the big topic for tomorrow – electronic commerce.

In all its guises and with all of its potential, the electronic trading of products, services and information will be a revolution. The opportunities are so vast in scale they are literally impossible to envisage. Technology has at last overtaken human and corporate imagination.

The key is to cut through the supplier and consultancy hype to discover the ideas and action that will drive *your* company forward and profit from the opportunities. E-commerce must be broken down into specific projects, and it must be done quickly.

The consequences of inaction will be serious. Just look at the effect that reward cards are having on traditional credit cards.

The IT director must take the initiative. Surrounded by a few, carefully selected experts who can translate technology into English, they should blaze a trail to their CEO and board. They must become the default source of ideas and information. Any IT department bypassed in this area will be bypassed forever.

Your CEO may be confused – you must provide all the answers, and make sound business cases for investment. The two strategic business drivers are simple – corporate pain and pleasure. Threat and opportunity.

Schedule a presentation to your board on this subject – go and see your CEO now. There are no easy answers, but paint the possibilities:

- This is the future – and it is coming, fast.

- What new markets would you like to trade in? The entry barriers just came down.

- What new countries would you like to trade in? The world just got smaller.

- What new customers would you like trade with? They just got closer.

- Your corporate brand is now your web-site – there are thirty million sites and this will double in the next twelve months – why should customers visit yours?

- How closely are you working with your marketing and PR departments?

- What are your competitors doing? Remember their number and type are growing all the time.

What an opportunity for the IT director to lead this process of business discovery and vision. Involve all of your people in forming ideas for action – focus on one or two and make a sound business case for investment. Try things out – your competitors are doing just that.

Picture the little child paddling at the seashore. See the wave form behind, some way off at first, then growing higher, faster and nearer. Watch it rise, and crash down, swamping everything in its path. The child is soaking. They do not know what has happened, but start to laugh. Don't let that child be you and your organization. If you do, your shareholders won't find it quite so funny.

17 | Euro ready – coming or not?

Vote however you wish, believe whatever you want, and call it what you will – the 'Euro' is coming. Clouded in political argument and emotion, IT directors want to know what is really going on, and what it means for their department and organizations.

Consider the horror of suddenly having to deliver ten or more major IT projects simultaneously within the space of eighteen months. Add to this significant business change and upheaval, and we should all be on red alert.

The Euro's arrival has crept up on us and has been largely ignored in favour of millennium work. The impact on IT systems is enormous and trivialized so much that the issue has been all but ignored by the vast majority. Many believe it to be far bigger than the Y2K problem.

For any organization, the transition to the Euro is essentially an enforced change management problem with its own timetable and deadlines, the implications of which vary, according to the enterprise's sector, own business strategy and the customer and competitor-driven pressure to be Euro friendly.

Over the next few years European customers are likely to switch their allegiances to neighbouring suppliers within Euroland. The pound is set to strengthen in January and this will further damage exports. British industry is threatened with being closed out.

Companies in EMU countries must at some time prior to 2002, prepare their systems to accept transactions in the Euro, either by switching to the Euro as the base currency or implementing a system with multi-currency facilities.

Technology must be exploited to maximize product visibility, gear up marketing, advertise across the internet and enable on-line ordering, i.e. getting into e-commerce, as quickly as the Euro gets into Europe.

The Euro, opportunity or threat aside, will hijack your IT strategy. This is really serious and the Euro has already claimed its victims; several financial institutions had to shelve major projects earlier this year to focus on this area.

Time waits for no one:

- Take a five-year view of the situation now – 2003 is our most likely entry year.

- Use the intervening period to best advantage, to rigorously assess the degree of change, formulate transition options and assess how the IT strategy is affected.

- Avoid embarking on long-term projects, which might be jeopardized in the event of Euro.

- Assess the size and complexity of changes and modifications required to applications and business data – focusing on your financial systems first.

- Ensure you know who will do this work – the Euro may well enforce a new skill crisis and staff shortage.

- Avoid at all costs being caught in the middle of a major project in 2002–3.

The Euro challenge is about enabling competitive advantage through effective use of technology whilst maintaining operations and switching the base currency for the entire organization.

The political debate is emotive and fun to watch. The commercial reality is that come 2003 many organizations are going to have to run faster then ever, just to stand still.

18 | IT director as king

The IT director is dead – long live the IT director. The disciples of doom are having a field day out there, widely, and wildly, predicting the end of the IT director. They are right in one sense – the role must change, but they are wrong that it will disappear.

Very wrong. As IT emerges out of the confusion and uncertainties of the last years of this century, we approach a major turning point in our history, and with it a real opportunity for IT directors to be influential power players.

The future IT director is business first, technology second. They are an IT literate business strategist, the chief executive's main advisor on how IT can drive the business and corporate vision, and a board-level member in their own right.

When looking for IT directors, organizations and head-hunters start with technology-related background and achievement. Relevant though this may be, it is of secondary importance to other skills. What are the skills of this new IT leader?:

- *Outstanding communications* – Ability to inspire and influence at all levels in their organization, including an ability to illuminate the most complex of issues to their business colleagues.

- *Charismatic leadership* – Earning respect, trust and following based on who they are, what they do and what they stand for, not from of their job title, size of office or hierarchical position.
  Successful future leaders will have that mysterious factor often referred to as charisma – combining a friendly nature with positive energy, magnetic personality and dynamic style.

Wider vision – Taking a wide perspective – forming external alliances with suppliers, networking with other IT directors, and contributing to, and learning from, the wider IT community.

Personal profile – Ensuring a high internal profile and visibility. Daily walks through their department and regular 'open forum' style meetings will be a priority.

Warrior – Playing the high stakes game, recognizing that politics are rife within each and every company. They will also have identified, and be close to, the real power players within the organization, keeping their friends close, their enemies closer.

Mind skills – Working to develop an already razor sharp mind and, recognizing the power of people's ideas and contribution as the most powerful weapon in success, ensuring creativity thrives.

Future IT leaders will make it happen, take action and lead by example. They will have a persistence to deliver and succeed, and a deep-rooted self-confidence and self-belief that transcends adversity – taking responsibility for things under their control and for their reactions to events they cannot influence.

Many people refer to these new dimensions as personal power – a combination of attitude, belief and behaviour.

It is within all of us to take this path – it may not be the easiest, it will certainly involve leaving comfort zones, but it is the most rewarding.

Design your personal destiny, and that of your department and people. Develop your personal power and ignite the human assets, potential and imagination that surround you. Make your future certain – shape it.

19 | A wolf in sheep's clothing

We must learn our lessons from the 'Article 2B' experience in the USA. This update of consumer law contains clauses that tip the balance in any software dispute heavily in favour of the vendor. It may be fun debating its innocent and irrelevant name, it will be far from funny if its one-sided and deep rooted consequences go on to become law.

Successful partnerships, and dispute resolution, should not depend on complex laws; they have to rely on trust and a determination to go forward.

You have to hand it to the American suppliers. This Article will mean they can do whatever they like. Bug-ridden software, withdrawal of support, licences revoked – that should all help our industry enormously.

One piece of good news from a UK point of view is our own CSSA (Computer Software Services Association), whom I hold in very high regard and would, I am sure, encourage a full debate before such a move was made over here.

And there's the rub. It is not as if this law has suddenly sprung up out of nowhere, it was first proposed four years ago. Yet it is only now that the 'user' community have started to have their say. Although one could argue that it is not in the IT leaders' interests to explore every piece of advance legislation, and they do have other things to occupy their minds, surely someone somewhere – especially in such a lobby-rich country as the USA – could have highlighted this change to the law, just a little earlier.

While there are many in our industry who notice, and comment on, such issues and their consequences, there is still deep rooted lethargy in many areas of corporate IT, both here and elsewhere in the world. Sometimes corporate IT appears trapped between our business masters, powerful suppliers, and our industry's poor reputation, influence and public track record.

We must become an industry that has no need for customer/supplier campaigns, new laws or thick contracts. Of course there will be disputes, as there are in all areas of commercial life. So let us focus on mediation, arbitration and resolution.

There are important specific and wider lessons to be learned from 'Article 2B'. It may be that we need a corporate IT advisory body, or IT directors 'think-tank' to comment on, and be consulted on, all proposed and new legislation.

Suppliers and their customers must work closer together in many areas – and not be driven further apart. The potential consequences of this new law on corporate IT departments are very serious, expensive and long term.

Let us hope that American groups like the Society of Information Management can now put a stop to this law, or at least make major amendments. If they do not, and all of this utter nonsense carries on, contracts will become thicker, lawyers ever richer, and the elements of trust between suppliers and customers all but destroyed.

'Article 2B' is not in anyone's interest. We must pull together to ensure that no such development happens here. We owe that much to IT directors everywhere, who spend enough time looking over their shoulders as it is, without having to worry about what new horrors may be just around the corner.

20 | Promises promises

Hands up all those IT directors who are confused about which database to go for? More to the point, how many of you feel the same anger and frustration that I do. The Comdex world IT trade exhibition is supposed to be associated with exciting positive developments, and answers. Not in database decisions, apparently.

The fact of the matter is this – Microsoft, the market in its clutches, has announced SQL Server 7.0. It looks a complex offering indeed. Oracle, on the other hand, is advising us to abandon operating systems and run our databases on something called 'raw iron.' Is this a genuine proposition? Or a desperate attempt to legitimize everything that was said about the demise of the PC?

What is the track record of these two companies? Microsoft does deliver – late and full of bugs. Will it be different this time round? Oracle do deliver – not always as intended. For example the widely hyped Network Computer has not taken off as intended, and is most often used to replace dumb terminals.

The poor IT director faces yet again a situation where their supposedly happy position at the pinnacle of the profession is threatened by a supplier industry who it is hard to believe has their best interests at heart.

The spite with which the campaign is being conducted, and it is the same with operating systems and the Java language, simply gives critics of the IT industry a field-day. They can say 'look, they don't even know what's going on in their own industry, what chance do the rest of us stand?'

What to do? Whom to believe? What chance accurate budgets now? The Oracle story is so compelling, like a lovely dream we keep waking up from. Such an approach would dramatically reduce total cost of ownership. On the other hand at least we know where we stand with Microsoft. We seem to accept that we are now Microsoft's software quality testers, and that we have to pay them for the privilege.

- Stay with your present strategy. Neither of these two announcements promise enough to make radical change.

- Write to your preferred supplier – Microsoft, Oracle or whoever, and seek written guarantees on delivery, dates and support.

- Watch for further announcements – if Oracle can tie in a couple of big partners things could change.

- Set your budgets for next year at the maximum cost.

While these non-announcements are made, IT directors continue to battle with more urgent matters. Just imagine if they treated internal customers in this way – they wouldn't survive, and rightly so. These continuing events have the atmosphere of at best raised expectations and more hype, at worst broken promises and deception.

If Microsoft and Oracle don't like those words let us raise this whole matter, with all its issues, into the open with a public debate – that is my challenge.

21 | Raising the standard

It's official – and public. Standardizing on one operating system, and PC configuration, saves money. Lots of it. Three cheers to Debenhams for achieving such an outstanding saving, being able to quantify it in real terms, and for going public. By moving its corporate desktop computers to a single operating system (Windows 95) it is saving £600 000 a year.

This is a classic example of changing the mindset from 'total' to 'true' cost of ownership – in which a company focus on their own position, costs and options in preference to the often conflicting information coming from the experts and benchmarks.

The arguments for standardization are many:

- Transformed improvement in the IT department's ability to resolve problems – as the support staff will not have to deal with many different configurations.

- More time can be spent addressing the people side – such as additional training.

- Quick win business solutions more easily deployed across an organization.

- Faster installation of PCs, both in local and network configuration.

- Trainees become productive more quickly, as they have less to learn.

- Clearer skill set within the IT department.

- More effective monitoring of network activity – increasing prevention, and reducing problems.

- Saved business time and frustration as one or two people resolve the problem, instead of the previous dozen who used to come and go.

In short, standardization combines the disciplines of the mainframe world (centralized data storage, single point administration, simple standardized terminals and capacity planning) with the flexibility of the PC platform.

If the advantages are so apparent, why do more IT departments not carry out this exercise? Simply because it is one of the most controversial projects that can be undertaken. The opposition comes from four angles:

1 The up front monetary, resource and skill investment can be high.

2 Other priorities are higher.

3 Internal IT disputes over the best operating system.

4 Business customers enjoy the freedom of 'personalizing' their own PC, or worse still ordering them direct, bypassing the IT department.

Once again, it is people, personalities and politics that hamper progress. There are powerful ways for IT departments to achieve their aims:

- Follow Debenhams example – quantify the savings in real terms.

- If business customers don't agree with the figures, have them independently audited.

- Seek independent advice from specialists in desktop support.

- Prepare a service charter showing the improved service that can be achieved, and the other projects that can also be done with the time saved.

Above all, stand up and be counted. If a business customer can find a PC cheaper from a local store let them buy it – clearly you cannot put it on the company's network (security), or incur the extra costs to support it.

Sometimes, unpopular as it may be, IT departments have to be cruel to be kind. Convince the right level of business customer, and make the project high profile, with clear, consistent communication and staged benefits.

The arguments for PC and operating system standardization is overwhelming, and presents a real opportunity to bury a long-held business myth – that IT departments do not think, and act, along hard business lines.

22 | Volume over value (pile 'em high, sell 'em cheap)

The culture pioneered by the direct PC suppliers has thrown up an unfortunate – and expensive – side effect. Lack of after-sales support. The annual *Computer Weekly*/KEW Associates *Quality of IT Suppliers Survey* (*Computer Weekly*, 3 December 1998) suggests that falling hardware prices, growing competition and lower margins have led to a focus on, and investment in, marketing, web-sites – and the sale. There appears to be little left in the pot to provide decent end-user support to the purchaser. Add to this the increasing complexity of hardware and software combinations and it is no wonder that purchasers feel abandoned once they have parted with their cash.

Help and service desk performance needs improvement, too, as the major suppliers find it increasingly difficult to service their growing user base. And it will worsen before it improves, as this PC growth is not being matched by parallel increases in consumer awareness and know-how.

There are some simple steps suppliers can take to transform the service:

- Publish clear guides on what to do, whom to call and what will happen when things go wrong.

- Commit to a service level agreement (SLA) on help-desk response and service – print it on the mouse-mat.

- Reintroduce the human element – have the phone answered by a person and not a machine, then schedule a call back time to suit the customer.

- Follow up each sale with a courtesy call to ensure everything is OK.

- Show an interest in fixing the human – not just machine – problem. Show that you care, in your voice, manner and whole approach.

- Talk in a language the caller understands. It is a real skill to be able to talk in plain English, without sounding patronizing. Training may be needed.

- Encourage your people to take ownership – half a caller's worry and concern can disappear if they feel someone is taking the problem off their shoulders.

These steps will all cost money, but will be a sound investment as customers realize (and tell others) that buying direct need not jeopardize high quality, after-sales service. Lessons can be learned from direct banking, and there will be opportunities for additional marketing, add-on sales and future upgrades.

In the future the problem will disappear, as a new generation of computer-literate children grow into purchasing maturity, with an in-depth understanding of the architecture of computers which some of us can only dream about.

Indeed, it is entirely possible that the whole future development of technology will be a far more interactive process between developers and customers, with direct support being provided by sophisticated user groups backed up by manufacturers.

For now, however, we must stop the cost of PC ownership soaring after the sale. Of course people realize that cheaper hardware comes with hidden extras. The introduction of SLAs will at least make it clear what those additional costs may be, and will allow a more balanced comparison between buying direct or through another route.

23 | **Where has all the training gone?**

Recent figures suggest that 90 per cent of IT projects fail to deliver any real benefit, while 40 per cent fail completely. They are late, over budget, not of defined or needed quality, or a combination of all three.

More frightening still, these are the figures we know about. Add in projects that collapse within companies, and are quietly brushed under the carpet to avoid bad publicity, and the trend is even more disturbing. As a country we spend millions of pounds on IT project management training every year, what is happening to all of that learning?

IT projects fail for many reasons:

- Ill-defined scope and aims.

- Lack of priority.

- Unclear ownership and accountability (IT and business).

- Resource (availability, quality, focus).

- Organizational politics (vying for power).

- Changes being made throughout the project.

- Blame culture (The highest priority is ensuring its not your fault).

- Lack of support for project manager.

- Poor communication.

The two most fundamental reasons, however, are that many senior managers do not appreciate:

1 All projects, every single one, are an ongoing balance and conflict between three priorities:

   (a) *Time* – the project must be completed within a specific timescale (e.g. millennium compliance);

   (b) *Cost* – the work must not cost more than a certain figure (e.g. many public sector projects);

   (c) *Quality* – It has to meet a certain specification (e.g. Channel Tunnel).

2 Project management is an attitude of mind, which goes beyond the simple ability to put together a plan that lists the principal activities in a neat order. It requires focus, dedication, interpersonal skills, humility, strong disposition and many other 'softer' skills.

The result is often a bunch of well meaning individuals doing their best to work through a technical, business and political minefield, in pursuit of some poorly defined goal, which keeps changing. This is totally unacceptable, and has gone on for far too long. There has to be a better way. Successful projects share similar characteristics:

- A clear priority in their organization.

- Well positioned in the 'eternal triangle' of time, cost and quality.

- Clear ownership by senior business and IT leaders, who together champion the project.

- An IT project management process.

- An agreed business case, clearly stating the business benefits and how they will be measured.

- Clear, detailed and signed off statement of requirements.

- Agreed change control procedure for changes to requirements.

- Risk analyses are completed – with every risk having an owner and contingency plan.

- All suppliers/sub-contractors are properly vetted and approved.

- Clear milestones that they are effectively tracked.

- The right resources to the project, particularly in testing and acceptance.

- Project managers receive positive and frequent support.

Make a New Year's resolution to do an honest, focused audit of all IT projects. Cut through the politics, measure them against the criteria for success, and champion a better way for your organization's future.

24 | A full twelve months

It would seem that the world is welcoming 1999 as a non-year, little more than an opportunity to reflect, as we countdown to the Millennium. In IT we must not fall into the same trap. The year 1999 must be the year when our young industry learns from our past, takes action on our present, and shapes a compelling future. We must use this year to maximum benefit. What will be the biggest issues for IT directors in the next twelve months?

The year 2000

The biggest challenge remains the unknown – no one can predict with absolute certainty what will happen, where and to whom.

We must focus on our own compliance, while working with, and helping, our supply chains, associates and customers. Although there will be problems, we should not make them self-fulfilling. The best way to create a food shortage is to predict one.

Staff retention and skills crises

This seems set to continue, and will be virtually recession proof. There will be more focus on permanent staff and the contractor market will reduce, but not collapse.

The three areas of focus are retention, motivation and cross-skilling. We need to attract more people into our industry, at all levels.

Supplier/customer relationships

This will grow in importance, as more relationships break down and companies revert to legal action.

Those companies that use independent arbitration and form trusted, powerful alliances with their suppliers, based on trust, clarity and communications, will save a fortune in time, money and resource.

The perception, and business alignment, of IT departments

In 1999 IT should work to be seen as core to business strategy and success, and we must work to increase IT presence at board level. IT and IT directors need to gain the recognition needed to enable business advantage.

IT remains the biggest enabler of competitive advantage, and is core to many companies.

The future role of the IT director

IT directors should ensure they are communicating the business benefits of IT throughout their organization, and, in particular, with the board and CEO. They should aim to build trust, and a personal rapport, at all levels.

Provided they take on the new skills needed, the future is bright for IT leaders. Indeed, this is imperative if 1999 is to be the turning point that we all desire.

In IT, let us ensure that 1999 is not remembered as a non-year, or worse still, as a countdown to disaster. Let this be the year when IT is no longer seen as a program, a line of code or a calculation, but rather a vision, a positive picture and personal experience.

There are many things to fear in the twelve months ahead, but we must not be fearful. To achieve this, I call on IT leaders, everywhere. Will you please stand up; your people need you.

25 | **The lessons of success**

Many congratulations to everyone involved in the New Year Euro project, which involved the biggest system upgrades ever seen in the City. It was by anyone's standards, a resounding success.

The loudest, and proudest, voices of praise came from the firms and financial regulators, many of whom cite this project as an example of what is really possible when business and IT objectives, people and processes are in harmony.

How may people expected such a successful outcome? And how much of the media was waiting for a disaster story to report? Sad indictment as it is, this project's lack of high-level national coverage is indicative of its success.

A failure would have made a higher slot on the national news. All the potential was there. The investment, scale and importance of this project, to so many companies, were awesome:

- It was totally date dependent, so could not be delayed.

- The systems had to work, or companies would lose millions, customers and credibility.

- The whole of Europe was watching – London is the leading trader in the Euro.

- The political dimension was present, with sceptics waiting to pounce on delay or collapse.

- The project went live at the start of a new year – every project manager knows the dangers of that – with the reliance on staff working over a holiday period.

What were the critical success factors that made this project overcome these challenges? What lessons can we learn in IT project management, business/IT cooperation and large-scale IT public relations? From talking with some of the key people involved, the following six traits ran through the various projects:

1 *Ownership.* Clear on all aspects of the project, from start to finish, across all areas, including commitment from the highest levels.

2 *Focus.* Never losing sight of the live date – one analyst told me it was like preparing for the first night of a play, there would be a paying audience, so the play simply has to be ready. Difficulties may happen along the way, but they are always overcome.

3 *People.* Advance planning on people's needs, accommodation and incentive payments, later time, off etc.

4 *Collective responsibility.* There were only a few isolated examples of people involved predicting problems in advance – unusual for such a large-scale project. The overall PR was excellent.

5 *Shared experiences.* Companies helped each other by cooperating on common issues and information.

6 *Public relations.* Business leaders involved were very quick to stand up and hail the project as a resounding success – IT people can shout from the rooftops about the good work we do, but, we will never carry such an impact.

We should take on board not only the specific lessons from projects such as this, but also the overall experience, approach and outcome.

At a time when negativity continues to surround us, let this experience remain with as a clear, positive, object lesson of what can happen when hearts and minds work together.

26 | So much more than money

One of the biggest questions facing all IT directors is how to avoid the staffing boom and bust cycle. Our industry suffered greatly through the downsizing of the last recession, and has paid the price over the last few years as the number of jobs has vastly outnumbered available people.

The latest *Computer Weekly* employment survey concludes that salary and overall financial package is the top consideration for people moving job. However, the survey reveals the two main reasons people stay in a job are:

1 'An interesting job' – 9 out of 10.

2 'Feeling valued' – 8 out of 10.

Ability to communicate well is the most important skill for a long-term career.

What are the lessons to learn from this information?:

- Attracting staff is not enough. It costs three times as much to recruit a member of staff as it does to replace them, so the emphasis on motivation, skill and personal development should continue.

- Be aware of why people are joining you (as well as why they leave) – is it really salary, location, security? Play on the reason, increasing its profile in future campaigns.

- Now is the time to invest in home-grown talent, and in staff retention. Continue to demonstrate that people are valued all the time, not just when they are in short supply. Address cultural change, skill and personal development.

- Contractors still have an important role to play. Now is a good time to decide which skills should be kept in-house and which can be outsourced – be absolutely clear on this in every-day operations and over time you will avoid the contractor reliance that seriously hurt many IT departments in 1998.

- Ensure you have a skills/staff database in place, especially if you are increasing permanent staff. This is crucial if you want to avoid realizing you had contractor reliance – after the contractor has left!

- Work with your HR department to develop a new people strategy that meets the real needs of your department, company and people in the next two years.

- Motivation is key. People will be more effective when they want to come to work, and enjoy being there.

- Many IT directors started to address motivation and morale for the first time during 1998, and these people projects will be coming to fruition in 1999.

However, be cautious. There are so many surveys these days; results from one or two can be confusing. There will always be regional, seasonal and business sector variations. Take note of overall trends, of best practice from other companies, but focus on your own realities.

Everyone is clear about one thing – we all talk about it, write on it, and agree with the fundamental premise. People are your company's number one asset, and with interesting work, feeling valued and communication coming to the fore in this survey, now is an excellent time to demonstrate that in practice – in your leadership style, department and company.

27 | League table 2000!

Last week The Prime Minister made a keynote speech about the millennium bug. It was high on facts, good on detail, but backfired on impact. The majority of papers only carried the first paragraph of the press notice – namely that Mr Blair has put local authorities on a warning...poor performers would be 'named and shamed' in June if they did not get their act together. These were the wrong words to use.

Action 2000 suggests that 50 per cent of 'small businesses' have not yet started, and that 15 per cent of councils need to do more. How will the publication of a 'league table' in June really help? Apparently it is so that 'councils and the public can judge progress for themselves'. What if my council is bottom? Are they relegated? Or do I rush to move house to a more compliant neighbourhood? The Y2K blame culture bandwagon is rolling early.

IT directors are up against it, from every angle, in every company. Local government, in particular, unable to afford high salaries, has suffered more than most from the skill shortages, pressures on time and priorities.

The big question is – will these comments assist local governments and small businesses with their compliance? The short answer is no. The danger is that these well used 'soundbites' will have other consequences:

- Anyone worried about their compliance will run for cover.

- More will sit and wait for things to go wrong – before suing someone.

- The tabloids, pencils already sharpened to name the first IT director responsible for any serious Y2K problems, may go to press early.

- Hard working IT directors will feel let down at a time when they need support.

The truth is that no one in the government, public or private sectors can predict with any great accuracy what will happen and what the consequences will be.

Forget league tables, lets talk harsh realities. If you still feel you haven't taken sufficient action you must, at the very minimum:

1 Perform a risk audit on all areas that might be affected – including your suppliers.

2 Identify the problems and assess business impact – in priority order.

3 Appoint a responsible person to own the project, and give them the authority and resources they need.

4 Recognize the need for damage limitation/contingency if all areas cannot be fixed in time.

5 Be prepared to seek external advice if you cannot come up with an achievable timescale internally.

6 Prepare your customers – tell them if you know of any areas which might not be fixed in time.

7 Seek external compliant facilities (bureaux, etc.) for any mission critical areas which may not be ready.

8 View this as potentially a major business continuity problem.

Let us hope that our leaders, newspapers and parliament carry this debate beyond the soundbites, political one-upmanship and dunces cap brigade. There is too much at stake for that.

28 | The elusive balance

As pressure grows on IT departments to become more business aware, customer-focused, and to take on new, 'softer' skills, let us not forget the importance of technology, and the people we rely on to make that technology work.

As we move out from behind the massive mainframes, lines of code and take our rightful place at the heart of organizations, it is easy to forget the importance of technical knowledge, skills and people.

Gone are the days when our careers are made by hardware track record, and for IT directors, leadership and communication abilities are more important than knowledge of software strategies.

Applied throughout an IT department, however, there is a risk that the swinging pendulum will move too far away from technical focus. Whether these skills and tasks are outsourced or kept in-house, IT directors and their leadership team need to retain overall control of *all* activities. The fact is that IT departments need a good balance of hard and soft skills, and people.

IT directors may need to work with their HR departments to provide a more flexible approach, perhaps two streams, one technical and the other more business/customer oriented:

- People should be able to progress within each stream and favour their natural inclination.

- Any competency based training system should be amended to reflect this new approach – rewards should be based on success at primary skills.

- Salary reviews should be equal and reflect equal contribution.

- Technical people need to have some knowledge of their business, and the wider picture. Make it clear the minimum that is expected of people in these areas.

- This year the people focus is moving away from recruitment, towards retention and motivation. Too much time and money has been invested in technology skills to risk losing them, and this new approach to recognition will help reduce staff turnover.

- Technical ladders can be put in place whereby people are promoted without having to become people managers, which is often a technical person's downfall.

Skill teams are a powerful way of achieving this. Allocating people from both streams to projects ensures a balance of the right abilities and knowledge. This produces a profile, which is both deep in one or two key technical skills, and broad across a wide mix of technology and interpersonal skills.

These skill teams, and this overall approach, can be extended to include contractors and third-party suppliers. When done in conjunction with a skill database, this will assist in strategic decisions on what should be done in-house, and what work should be outsourced. It also helps keep a closer track on key skills, and shortfalls, on an ongoing basis.

I am a leading advocate of IT departments running like a business, communicating in English, and working hard on their marketing and perception. However, in achieving these vital milestones, let us not forget that we need technical skills as well, and to recognize the contribution made by everyone.

29 | **Murders and acquisitions**

As mergers and acquisitions continue to grow in number, and scale, many people talk about giants learning to dance. In the world of IT, however, where it is very rare for technical and information considerations to be taken into account until the major decisions have been made, those giants are far more likely to collide.

For many reasons (shareholder value, possible last minute collapse and legal considerations), talks on formal alliances and take-overs are officially kept secret until they are completed. What are the implications for IT directors, and departments, of such actions, and the secrecy involved?

IT is a significant area of spend in all organizations, and therefore a target for sizeable savings. While the CEOs, financial and legal teams are making decisions behind the scenes, who is considering the IT context, issues and implications?

IT directors are usually involved after a decision has been made, and then find themselves having to deliver on the savings that have already been decided. Imagine the shock for the IT director when they discover:

- The new company has significant Y2K problems.

- The two infrastructures are incompatible.

- Each company has adopted different telecom strategies.

In addition, the IT leader is put on the back foot. They are immediately faced with new priorities, people issues, and having to make fast, reactive decisions. At best they will have to make significant savings, at worst a major round of redundancies, or even a site closure. Either way, there is a real danger that focusing on these new areas will delay business critical projects.

Then there is the politics. No matter how many studies are carried out, or reports written, mergers inevitably mean an immediate power struggle, as the cake is divided. With acquisitions, the bought company almost always ends up fighting for survival, as the acquirer is so often the winner.

In short – the IT perspective is rarely considered in mergers and acquisitions until it is too late. Politics then play a major role in decisions, and the consequences are usually short-term, head-count savings as opposed to real long-term benefits and strategic growth. There has to be a better way for everyone concerned.

IT directors, or at least the IT implications, need consideration up front. This would enable:

- Real cost saving decisions to be made.

- A professional assessment of IT compatibility.

- Advance notice of the major issues.

- Buy in from the IT director, who will have to oversee implementation.

- The overall value of any deal being clearer.

All IT directors need to convince their CEO of their value in the event of merger discussions, or at least make the board aware of the key issues to address in such an event.

IT is core to most companies, and must be considered with the same independence, depth and professional approach as other areas. Taking advance, realistic decisions is critical to mergers and acquisitions achieving the long-term success that everyone involved sets out to achieve.

30 | Take control of your own destiny

Any organization that outsources its complete IT department is taking enormous risks. Those that do so for anything longer than two years are committing commercial suicide. It is like giving away your crown jewels. The argument that it reduces hassle and allows an organization to 'focus on core business' may apply to short-term arrangements, but not to five- and ten-year deals.

If your company is serious about shaping its future, it will already take IT seriously – in finance, strategy and attitude. Forward thinking companies put IT at their very heart, and conduct business around this core investment. The direct financial services have proved this – transforming whole business sectors, while improving customer service and retaining the flexibility to add new products and services faster than their traditional rivals.

If you need any further convincing, look at the problems that arise in long-term outsourcing arrangements. Why does this happen? What goes wrong?:

- The business loses control over its IT and corporate strategies.

- The world is changing faster than ever – no one can predict what IT will be like in five years.

- Companies need the ideas and innovations of their own people to use technology to long-term advantage.

- Suddenly the original financial savings do not look so attractive, as costs rise, disagreements grow, and the focus moves to the relationship, rather than the competitive advantage.

- Long-term outsourcing is often done for the wrong reasons – short-term cost savings or pleasing political masters.

There is nothing wrong with outsourcing as a strategy. It is total outsourcing for long periods of time that is destined for disaster. There are other ways. To decide the right approach for your company, ask the right questions, and involve your business partners:

- Which areas provide real value to your organization?

- Where are you having the biggest problems of staff skills, training and retention?

- Which activities do your staff find motivating – and which demoralizing?

- What areas give you the greatest problems, and headaches?

Find out what your peers in similar organizations have done – seek out advice on best practice. Look at the evidence – what seems to work, and what does not?

Successful outsourcing needs choice, clarity and control. Your organization must choose what is right for them, over what period of time, and in what areas. IT services must be clear for the business customers they serve – who does what, and takes responsibility when things go wrong? (The acid test of all outsourcing agreements.)

Finally, never hand over total control – and make sure that any and all agreements reflect this. Allocate a project manager to oversee your suppliers, ensure a smooth transition, and ongoing quality of service.

IT departments must retain flexibility, and avoid restrictive long-term agreements. This may be achieved through short-term arrangements, or by outsourcing selected services on a modular basis. Both ways will ensure that you retain focus, accountability and control of your own destiny.

31 | Post non-recession budget

What will the budget hold for corporate IT, and IT leaders? I recently read that our economy is set for a 'soft landing' – meaning that we are just coming out of a period of zero growth and set to see the economy strengthen again. IT directors will be delighted that we are moving out of the recession we never had!

It was only a few months ago that we couldn't find the skills we needed and IT strategies were being altered to fit the knowledge we had available. Any sign of stability is welcome.

These strong economic messages, combined with the inevitable entry into the Euro and post-Y2K contingency and legal issues arriving in spades, means that this period of stability will be shorter than we wanted, and needed.

Good news for recruitment companies bad news for IT directors. The focus on retention, motivation and cultural transformation must grow, as these are the most powerful antidotes to avoid high staff turnover. Get these right today, and you won't go into recruitment overdrive tomorrow.

IT directors have three areas of interest in the budget – their personal income/finances, corporate issues and how it will affect their departments.

A few predictions:

- With a few notable exceptions, a safe budget. Gordon Brown has plenty of money available.

- Married allowance abolished.

- Lower tax rates extended.

- Major increase in inheritance tax.

- Capital allowances will be increased to encourage new technology companies.

- Bigger incentives for relocation in Enterprise Zones.

- At the other end of the scale, capital gains tax will rise.

The reduced lower scale tax should encourage IT departments to look at long-term training plans for new and inexperienced people – perhaps an in-house coaching academy for IT skills. IT departments could forge links with local schools and universities to launch this.

We must also find a way to bring new people into IT at all levels. There are many people who want to enter IT, but do not know how.

With IT salaries being higher than many other disciplines, any budget that hits the higher earners will lead to greater internal pressures on compensation, alternative methods of reward and yet more debates around performance related pay.

If you are about to launch a new technology company – wait until after the budget, if you are about to sell – do it today!

IT directors should seek out and encourage new technology companies to partner. Venture marketing will increase – powerful alliances between IT departments and new technical companies. In exchange for funding an IT department has exclusive use of the technology.

Many of these will depend on securing greater IT investment in your company. A strong economy will support your arguments for greater funding. The downside of any growth will be a return to the boom periods, and more skill shortages.

Enjoy the sanity while it lasts!

32 | Linux leaves school

If it works, don't use it. This philosophy seems rife in the IT industry's short history, with new software, often shareware, capturing people's imagination more than the tried, tested and documented solutions. Nowhere is this better illustrated than with Unix and Linux. When first introduced, Unix was on everyone's lips. True, it was unreliable, but what is that when compared to the excitement of something fresh, an alternative to the establishment.

As the Unix world stabilized and support improved, interest started to decline. Enter Linux – the freebie operating system to end all other operating systems. It was new, it was free, but most of all it was sexy. No support, no manuals, no real structure – what an excellent system to adopt. The fact that hidden costs of ownership soared seemed irrelevant.

Who could have predicted its phenomenal growth? Least of all Hewlett-Packard and IBM, who last week broke supplier ranks to provide service and support around the Linux operating system. Why? A mix of three reasons:

1 To take hold of, and control, an open product, by introducing proprietary versions.

2 As recognition of Linux's strength, and a genuine desire to invest in its future.

3 Out of pure fear – that their millions of investment were now being threatened by a maverick product that would clearly not go away.

The big question for IT directors and strategists is, what does it mean for us? Are we really going to throw out Unix or NT in favour of a piece of free software grown and developed by techies, or are the costs, reliability and ease of use going to improve, to make this a serious strategic option?

Last week's developments alone do not justify a change in strategy, however, they do call for a close watch on the future.

- How will Microsoft react?

- Will Linux now follow Unix and become yesterday's news – prompting something newer?

- Where will the major Linux applications come from?

The IT press was full of praise for developers. David has beaten Goliath, or at least persuaded the bigger man to adopt, and look after, him. The developers' world was at once both cheering and depressed. Glad that Linux's strengths have at last been realized, sad that its image is likely to change forever, a poacher no more.

These are the wrong considerations. The day for true celebration will be when an operating system delivers proven, measurable and long-term business benefits.

Go and ask your business customers for their reaction to this week's news, they will not show any interest. Tell them that this will lead to savings and better service in the future, they will walk away – they have heard it all before. But demonstrate it in practice – by turning Linux into a reliable, seamless and cost-effective infrastructure, saving real money – and you will start to receive their attention.

If Linux's destiny is to be so great, let it prove it on business territory.

33 | Future shock

See the future. It is Saturday 17 March 2000; you broke your millennium resolution not to bring work home, a long time ago. Here you are sitting in the lounge, listening to Mozart, and pondering four piles of paper. Which one to tackle first?

The first pile is quite small – just three A4 sheets of paper. This is the specification for your new Euro system, which has to be ready in six months, will cost three times as much as your Y2K compliance, and will eat up all of your most valued resource. With millennium compliance you made all of your legacy systems strategic, and so you realize that you will have to retain all those expensive contractors.

Your attention turns to the second file – more substantial than the Euro papers, in fact this one is positively bulging. The word 'litigation' is scrawled across the top in red, with the additional 'actual – for potential see separate file' underneath. This file contains all the legal disputes involving suppliers who failed to achieve Y2K compliance, causing major problems for your company as a result.

The third collection is a tall pile of notes, reports and printed e-mails. As you pick up the top piece of paper, a sense of foreboding passes over you. For this is the Y2K contingency file. All of those plans your company rushed to put in place in January 1999, when it realized it had no chance of meeting its deadlines. As a result, there are some reconciliation issues between the manual and automated systems. The paper you are holding is from your Financial Director, who wants to know where two million pounds has gone from the accounts system. Stupid man, why does he get involved in such detail?

Your feet move uneasily, reluctant to surrender the enormous fourth group of papers they were using as a footstool. This pile is a positive tower, nearly three feet tall, by far the largest. It represents all the project and work requests from your business customers, backdated eighteen months while you worked on Y2K compliance. These are the documents that were delivered with positive glee, as your peers outside of IT made up for lost time. No excuses now, they said, so here you are. Still, they must all be important, as they are all 'priority one'.

What a nightmare vision! Surely such events could never happen – or could they? We are only now beginning to realize the scale of work involved for the Euro, and some Y2K experts have openly stated they will be available as expert witnesses for Y2K litigation. Many companies are simply not Y2K compliant, and are relying on contingency as their only hope. Finally, almost every company I know has outstanding project requests, and these grow every day.

What to do now?

Your choice – reach for the tissues, or rewrite the future.

34 | Enough is enough

Workplace bullying has recently received a lot of coverage:

- What is it?

- Does it exist?

- Does it happen in your organization or IT department?

Bullying occurs when one person in a position of power tries to control, or undermine, another person using aggressive physical and psychological strategies, on a consistent basis. The term 'bully' describes a range of behaviours, from a persistent unwillingness to recognize performance, loyalty and achievement, to repeated critical remarks and humiliating and overtly hostile behaviour such as shouting at an employee in front of colleagues.

There is widespread controversy on the subject, with expert opinions sharply divided. At the one extreme, the last year has seen thousands come forward and claim they have suffered, while opponents claim it is people misreading normal professional behaviour, that business is a hard world anyway, and that many of these individuals are merely attention seeking, or playing victim.

Tim Field (www.successunlimited.co.uk), author and expert on business bullying, cites the following precipitating circumstances for bullying to thrive:

- Stress – becoming a major issue for IT leaders (the Health and Safety Executive estimate the cost of stress to the UK economy is £4 billion a year).

- Speed of change.

- Not being valued in an organization – IT still has a poor image among many business leaders.

- A culture of long hours – working late still attracts serious brownie points in too many companies.

- Information overload.

- Pressure of work.

- Uncertainty – Threats of outsourcing, and needing to retrain in the right skills.

This list puts IT departments at high risk of bullying behaviour, and it gets worse. The most prevalent reason for bullying to start is when things go wrong, and with eight out of ten IT projects failing, and a few shaky infrastructures around, there is wide scope for blame, protecting of backs and hunting out scapegoats.

One could argue that IT departments themselves are being corporately bullied by their business customers, who are constantly demanding a better, quicker and more effective service, at a cheaper cost!

In IT, we continue to suffer from a techie, macho image. Although this is changing, with more women coming into the profession and a sharper focus on interpersonal, marketing and softer skills, are we changing fast enough?

Not only must IT leaders address these cultural issues, they must constantly review their management styles, to ensure they are not abusing their positions of power. And, when someone comes forward for help, leaders must lend a sympathetic and understanding ear.

Everyone has a right to carry out their work without being harassed, or having their self-confidence or self-esteem undermined.

Many people find the whole subject of bullying incomprehensible, funny even, and if that applies to you, ask yourself the following question before you put your head back in the sand: 'Have I seen anyone being treated unfairly, aggressively even, on a regular basis?' If the answer to that is yes, do something about it, and do it now.

35 | Bargain basement

I find the term small to medium enterprises a little patronizing, however the Enterprise Resource Planning giants such as Saap and Baan do not share my view, and are now courting this lucrative market for new customers.

These 'SME' companies now have a three-way choice between bespoke development, off-the-shelf packages and this new offer, which is, in effect, cut down versions of larger solutions, available on a rented basis.

The dangers of in-house development are well documented, with the vast majority of projects failing to achieve required objectives. Software packages have not proved to be the panacea that customers hoped and vendors promised, mainly because they are rarely taken on board as intended, as packages.

What are the issues behind this new offer? Integration is good, integration works. No one wants a whole range of disparate systems, handling different parts of their business, none of which talk to each other, and these large-scale systems were designed to overcome this. At last there was a single system that would do it all!

As with everything that sounds so easy when the supplier is talking, it is not quite so simple once the contract is signed, and many bigger users of such systems have hit problems. They found that, like the difference between buying an integrated hi-fi system and separates, not all parts of the system are best of breed. Many compromises had to be made to do things as the software dictates.

There is naturally huge reluctance by the manufacturers to change the systems, as they are so huge, complex and interdependent. Users of enterprise resource systems have also found:

- A customer perception of putting all their eggs in one basket.

- Problems with the cost and implementation difficulties of these systems, requiring as they do major reviews of business processes if they are to be effective.

- Such systems are as much about cultural issues, as technical ones, yet they are often left to the IT department as if it was just another system.

There will be plenty of marketing literature telling you how wonderful these systems are, but what are the dangers?:

- The company being forced down a road of dependence, and road of no return?

- Up-front costs are competitive, cost of support and skills not so cheap. The real investment should be looked at over the life-cycle of the whole system.

- A cut-down version may give even less incentive to view these systems as business changing opportunities.

- A plethora of different versions may arise, tailored to the SME market.

The best solution may be to integrate best of breed systems for each business function, developed or sourced according to the commercial need within your organization. If you do decide to go with the new ERP offering, proceed with caution. Be aware of the scale and long-term cost of the offering, regardless of its apparent sudden appearance in the early summer sales.

36 | A time to talk

What have the Melissa virus, Y2K compliance, stress among IT directors, IT project failures and the GCHQ, all have in common? They are all shrouded in secrecy. Everyone knows they are major issues, all IT directors acknowledge they exist and are having a major effect on organizations, but not their own. Very few will stand up and talk about it.

Understandable, really. The faith, support and money of CEOs, customers and shareholders is not best encouraged by companies wasting money, being threatened by mission-killing viruses, or seen to fail.

On the other hand, every IT department is being hit by the same challenges and problems, and the many reasons behind them. Some of the important issues that do not receive a wide enough airing are:

- *Y2K*. The *real* state of compliance.

- *Projects*. Major business projects are still seen as purely IT projects. They are not prioritized by their board, lack clear objectives and business partners are not taking ownership of their responsibilities.

- *Business PC developments*. There is now more IT work being done outside of IT than within it, through so called power users. This work will inevitably end up in the IT department.

- *Skills*. Contractor reliance and having to pay premium prices for selective skills. Battling against the head-hunters who are always on the phone.

- *Stress*. At a recent conference of over 200 IT leaders, I asked how many believed stress was a major issue for IT directors – over 90 per cent of the room. I then asked who had, personally, suffered from stress in the last three months. No one!

We all know these issues are happening, that they are affecting many companies, but we continue to keep so much to ourselves. There are some ways to take this forward, on a local level:

- Form a strategic alliance with a company of a similar size to yourselves – to meet, compare progress and share problems and solutions.

- Create a feeling of openness and trust among your top team – even within organizations, if the culture is not right, people will not share information and opinions.

- Form strategic partnerships with your suppliers to keep track of the real information you need. Be wary of vendors and suppliers claiming to have the answers to everything, though!

- There is, however, a crying need for a no-risk, open and trusted forum that will allow IT directors to share their concerns, and to help each other.

- Just imagine how much money, time and effort we would all save if we could help each other more. An exchange of possible solutions, of ways forward. Of course, what works in one organization may not work in another, and many approaches do give strategic advantage, but there are enough areas of common problems and interest to benefit from sharing more.

- Next time you are networking with other IT directors, and swapping business cards, I encourage you to share with your new colleague the biggest challenge you have in your department, and ask them if they can help you.

37 | Chaos or freedom?

Incredible as it may seem, more IT development takes place outside of corporate IS departments, than within. The growing PC population and increasing number of 'power users' have created an enormous and mission threatening challenge to many organizations. This is how it happens:

- Disenchanted with the out-of-date online applications, and not understanding the IT project submission process, the user develops their own local solution, to meet their particular needs.

- They are very proud of this, and soon pass it round the department, and company, so that more people can use it.

- It quickly becomes a strategic application, being enhanced all the time.

So what you may ask. We supply the machines, the easy to use applications, and if business people choose to develop their own solutions, that is relieving the burden from IT departments. Also, PCs are integral to many people's work. These are compelling arguments, however:

- Such developments rarely have any documentation, so the original developer quickly becomes the local help desk, which is fine until they leave the department, company, or it becomes too much for them.

- Such developments seldom follow any standards or procedures.

- Ownership is unclear – until something goes wrong, when IT own it, even if this is the first they have heard of the application (what a lame excuse!).

- Business people start to spend more time playing with applications than doing the job for which they were employed.

- Putting such applications on local area networks – as is often requested – can bring down other systems.

- Word quickly spreads that IT is slow at doing things, compared with Mike in marketing who will run you off an Excel macro in two days. Mike then becomes his own IT service department, and doesn't he love it!

The hidden costs associated with this trend are enormous. These applications must be explained, supported and even integrated with existing systems.

There is no easy solution that solves all of the business, IT and financial concerns. However, action can be taken to minimize problems:

- Standardize on one office suite throughout your company.

- Document the number of user-developed applications in your organization by forming a group of senior and influential IT/business users.

- For each application, who owns it, supports it, and is there any documentation?

- Is the application used by more than one person, and is it mission critical? Prioritize your mission critical dependence/ exposure.

- As an IT department put standards in place for such development.

- Estimate the total cost of ownership of supporting these applications, and share this information with business users at all levels.

This is an emotive subject. PCs are there to be used; the keys are to appreciate this goes on, quantify its scale, and ensure good lines of communication between business and IT. If such developments go underground the problems are ten times worse.

38 | Twenty-first century people

What happens after what comes next? Post Y2K, will we return to 'normality,' (whatever that was) or will the whole compliance activity, combined as it was with business projects being delayed or shelved, and skill shortages, dictate a different approach?

Over the next three weeks some of the main issues will be explored, with emphasis on:

- *People* – Leadership, attracting new staff into IT, retention, skills, culture, and personal issues such as stress.

- *Partnerships* – Becoming a strategic asset at the heart of the company, office politics and perception, budgeting and project justification, suppliers and the concept of co-opetition (cooperating with your competitors in certain areas).

- *Performance* – Programme delivery, strategic infrastructures, adopting new technology and running IT along business lines.

People mean business, they are your company, and they are the difference between success and failure. The business process reengineering days are long gone, successful companies are gaining their staff's commitment, shared vision and loyalty.

Retention of key staff

The problem with staff turnover is losing staff you most want to retain. You know who you want to keep – invest in them, ask them why they stay with you (as opposed to waiting until they resign and asking them why they are leaving!).

Cultural transformation

Do your people want to come up work? Is there a positive buzz around your department, or is it a case of keep your heads down, avoid blame and get out the door as fast as possible at home time? Take this issue seriously before it bites you where it hurts. Put in place a set of values based on openness, learning and integrity.

Attracting new staff into IT

Everyone agrees it is much needed, how many are doing it? Look beyond the traditional IT CVs and bring in fresh blood, already trained in the skills you need.

Leadership

Gone are the days when respect is earned by shouting or a big office. You are no longer a fancy job title, or even what you say – you are what you do. We are our behaviour. Leaders are made, not born. For IT directors, management as we know it is dead.

Strategic skills

Make a strategic decision on which skills you will keep in-house. Outsource on a modular basis. Doing this will give people clearer roles, reduce reliance on contractors, save money and help to avoid a crisis during the next peak in skill shortages.

Personal issues

Take your health seriously, and be aware of who is suffering from stress, and burnout, around you. Don't just talk about it next time you arrive home too late to see your children before they go to bed, take steps now to get your life in balance between home and work. Also, keep learning and developing. Fewer people are staying in the same job, or company. Your future success will depend on you, your attitudes, abilities and skills.

Above all, look forward not back, face up to tough personal and people decisions, and commit to make the effort that is needed. Otherwise that effort will become tomorrow's struggle.

39 | Twenty-first century partnerships

What happens after what comes next? As we make our final preparations for the new millennium, what will be the main challenges for the IT director and departments, in the world beyond? Last week we looked at the much quoted, but little acted on, importance of people. I often write about releasing human potential, and will continue to do so until more companies take positive action in this area, which includes far more than just achieving Investors in People (IIP) accreditation.

The next issue we will focus on is performance – programme delivery, strategic infrastructures, the adoption of new technology and running IT along business lines.

This column looks at internal and external relationships, and how to transform them into trusted partnerships.

Post-millennium projects

Many business managers within your organization will share the IT director's joy at seeing the end of the Y2K problem, but for different reasons. The IT director has no excuses anymore, and it is time to do some real work. All of those projects that have been put on hold will now surface. It's payback time.

This potentially huge workload must be identified early, along with resource implications.

Budgets

There is a real danger that CEOs will conclude that as 70 per cent of IT budgets have been spent on Y2K, the department can now run on 30 per cent of their costs. The new project demands will help the IT director in this regard, but increasing discretionary spend will take sound business arguments.

Relationships

Y2K work has built a barrier between many businesses and IT service providers. This must now be removed. Revisit your service charters, identify the good communicators around you, and be proactive in ensuring regular contact with business customers when things go right, as well as wrong.

Strategic business asset

Now is the time to focus on investment, not spend, to forever shake off our image of being a drain on the company. Present a compelling vision to your board on the business opportunities post Y2K.

Personal influence

As an IT director much of your success or failure comes down to interpersonal communications. Take networking and office politics seriously. Develop your negotiation skills.

Suppliers

Now is the time to review your suppliers, both numbers and relationships. The fewer suppliers the better and putting in place a preferred supplier scheme can lead to less hassle and significant rewards.

Be ready for post-Y2K disputes with non-compliant suppliers, by putting in place effective arbitration procedures now. Signing up to such initiatives as the Millennium Accord will save much wasted time and money later.

Co-opetition

This new concept states that every competitor is also a potential partner. Companies that put aside competitive differences and focus on areas of non-conflicting mutual interest are benefiting enormously. Tesco and Esso used to be rivals, and are now working closely together. Look at your suppliers, other companies in your industry, and beyond. The opportunities for strategic alliances are many, the benefits for those who move quickly, enormous.

40 | Twenty-first century performance

It's official – the cute, cuddly and colourful millennium bug will not be in the shops for Christmas. Indeed, it is an endangered species. As the clocks at last bring in 2000, how many IT departments will go the same way? Unless you are your company's true IT provider of choice, you are at risk.

In the last of three columns focusing on the main issues for the IT director, we look at performance. If all your projects go in on time, to spec and cost, if your infrastructure is available 100 per cent and treated as strategic, and if new technology is delivering real, measurable financial benefits to your company's customers and shareholders, then read no further.

Management and control of the IT function receives scant attention against the exciting new worlds of digital convergence, e-everything and globalization. It is almost dismissed as being yesterday's news, rather than fundamental to everything an IT service provider delivers.

In the last seventeen years, we have spent millions on project management training yet eight out of ten IT projects fail – where has all the money gone? Technical infrastructures are now referred to as 'plumbing'. If my water and central heating systems worked with the same efficiency – a ten-second-response time to clean your teeth – I would seriously worry. Finally, are you adopting new technology in the right areas, and achieving fast results? Or are you being sold on the hype?

Of course many companies have tackled some or all of these issues, but they still haunt IT departments, in one form or another.

Projects

Prioritize all projects, and ensure each has clear business ownership (not tacit buy-in) and measurable benefits. Allocate a strong,
focused and fair-minded IT project manager. For big projects
avoid big bang, go live in phases on the way. Celebrate success,
communicate widely and above all else, focus on the outcome you
are trying to achieve – every day, at every milestone and with
everyone working on it. And forget benchmarking with function
point analysis – unless you have a lot of time to waste, and love
meaningless statistics.

Infrastructure

The bedrock of your business, and to be treated as such. It is a
strategic investment, and this must be translated into company
benefits at boardroom level. Your wires and cables are only as reliable as your customers think they are, so don't worry too much
about expensive measuring tools. And ditch meaningless benchmarking – unless you need the graph paper for your children to
draw on at home.

New technology

Recruit a futurologist whose role is to identify the new technologies that will work for your company. Make sure these add real,
fast and visible value. Enter into venture marketing partnerships
with suppliers, and look at what is working elsewhere.

Each of these suggestions are drawn from real IT departments
throughout the country, and they work. When at last these performance issues take their place in your IT history, let them be
remembered as an achievement, and not a legacy.

41 | Disaster reality

People tell us not to refer to 'problems,' only 'challenges.' Well, last week Richmond Events were faced with the challenge of a lifetime. The IT Directors Forum, one year in the planning, due to involve nearly 1000 people, and arguably the major event in the diary for IT directors, was cancelled with three days' notice.

At 4 pm on Bank Holiday Monday P&O informed Richmond Events that the *Oriana* ship, on which the event was due to take place, would not be available due to over-running maintenance work. In one phone call, the entire venue disappeared.

Their handling of this crisis is an object lesson for companies everywhere. The following day they contacted every speaker, exhibitor, delegate, journalist and sub-contractor involved.

It was not a simple or pleasant message to convey. Richmond pride themselves on the quality of their events, speakers and the influential level of their delegates. Everyone looks forward to this event, disappointment was guaranteed, and reactions unpredictable.

I received calls later on Tuesday from others who were due to speak/attend. One suggested that the event should take place a week later (making the assumption that 900 plus people would be available), another that Richmond should just book another venue, such as the Birmingham NEC (at two days notice), and by far the best reaction was the person who suggested the event should go ahead in dry dock! I suppose it would negate the need for an emergency drill.

Many people write about the theory of handling a crisis, few have to put it into practice. What are the key lessons to be learned from Richmond?

- *Speed of action.* Richmond could do nothing until Tuesday morning; everyone was contacted in one day.

- *Clarity of message.* The same message delivered in the same way, under high-pressure circumstance.

- *Professionalism.* It would have been easy to blame others, to express anger and disappointment – they did not.

- *Handling of press.* Press release issued at specific time to be in papers the following day. Clear cooperation with P&O on the message.

- *Working to a structured plan.* People telephoned in specific order, clearly noting when they could not reach the right person.

- *Understanding the reactions they would receive.* Including everyone's first thought – that this is a wind-up!

- *Total contingency.* Neil Tait, project manager for the event, travelled to Southampton, just in case anyone turned up. I hope there wasn't a ship waiting!

The key judgement on how a company handles a crisis comes a month after the event, when the urgency and emotion have passed, when they ask themselves what they could have done better, and when they suddenly realise they now have a master plan for handling any similar events in future.

I only hope, not least from a personal point of view that Richmond never has to go through this again. They think they had a problem, what about the new bow tie I bought!

42 | Avoiding the fault line

Television audiences simply can't have too many 'real-life' programmes thrown at them. Anything with conflict goes down particularly well. We have *Car Wars*, *Neighbours at War*, and it will be just a matter of time before we have 'IT Supplier Wars'.

As the potential areas for conflict, dispute and publicity soars, huge investments in time, money and resource are being focused on such relationship issues. And that is before the Y2K really takes hold. Just wait until January next year.

This depressing reality can be avoided. Not just by avoiding such fallouts, which have been covered in this column before, but after the disagreements, conflicts and threats begin. IT leaders and their suppliers have three alternatives to battle stations, expensive legal fees and avoiding the road of no return.

Mediation

The aim of mediation is for both parties involved to reach a mutually agreed, constructive outcome, achieved with the help of an independent facilitator. The main advantages of mediation are:

- Everyone agrees to try to reach such an outcome, which is positive in itself.

- Outcomes are likely to be bought in by all.

- The process often brings to the surface deeper issues that may not otherwise be identified.

Mediation involves some risk and investment:

- It is time-consuming, taking you away from core issues.

- The process depends on a degree of trust which may not be present.

- The mediator must be an independent third party – good people are not cheap.

Arbitration

Perhaps mediation has failed, the parties cannot afford the time, or the issues concerned need to be resolved quickly. The aim of arbitration is for an independent third party to look at the issues and facts, and listen to both parties, to make a decision that is binding on everyone involved.

This approach is often faster than mediation, is far more cut and dried than mediation, and parties involved often open up more when talking in private with a trained arbiter. The big danger with such an approach is achieving true and lasting win–win.

Arbitration is far preferable to court, provided everyone is sure it is the right issues that are being resolved.

Separation

I have often likened customer/supplier relationships to marriage. Entered into freely by two parties, success depends on compatibility, commitment and total trust. It disturbs me that many customers and suppliers do not sign contracts, in which case they are just living together. Nothing wrong with that in itself, but there will be far less incentive and legal obligation, to resolve disputes. Sometimes customers and suppliers cannot resolve their differences. No amount of talking, listening and independent help can take them forward. In this case separation may be the answer. Some companies simply cannot work together, and admitting this will avoid future hassle and problems.

Separation

Whatever you decide, always try to see things from each other's point of view, demonstrate total business acumen throughout, and keep all issues in perspective.

43 | E-mail rage

How did we ever manage without e-mail? How did people cope without their daily fix of words, communication and information?

Our in-trays seem to act like magnets, and there is little doubt that e-mails have improved our effectiveness. However, by speeding up the tempo, complexity and reactive pressure of business life, they have opened up new dangers.

Quite apart from the growth in paper as everyone prints them off, e-mails feed our reactive, rather than responsive behaviour, often fail to make the points intended, and are often used as an alternative to personal contact. In addition, there are growing moral, legal and corporate responsibilities.

Information on other companies

Such detail can, and has been, used in courts of law. Do not use e-mail to discuss competitors, potential acquisitions or mergers, or to give your opinion about another company. The word confidential simply does not apply to electronic communication; somebody else in your organization can always access it.

Information on individuals

Take great care, even with facts. Also, avoid providing references by e-mail.

Personal e-mails

Many companies are concerned about the growing numbers of non-work related correspondence. Often these will be through in-house bulletin boards. The key words here are guidelines and trust. Put in place a clear policy that gives some freedom, but people know their boundaries on time and content. There is a difference between such personal e-mails, and personalizing business correspondence. This latter approach should be encouraged, to make e-mails more friendly.

Aggressive e-mails

The biggest area of concern. Be aware of the power of the written word, and always read the finished mail through the eyes of the recipient.

It is one thing to misunderstand the sender's intent, quite another to deliberately attack someone by e-mail. Business bullying is now recognized by industrial tribunals as a form of illegal behaviour in itself.

Sexual harassment

The cases of this, and stalking over e-mail, are growing. It is now so easy to reach intended recipients. Company policy must be extended to include this area, and lead to dismissal. Encourage people to come forward with evidence, and make it clear that all e-mails are held on the mainframe or network after they have been written. This statement in itself will discourage most people.

Chain e-mails

Another growth area. These are at best unpleasant and at worst destructive in terms of time, volume of traffic and personal well being. Treat these very seriously, root out their origins, and put in place an address where recipients can send these. Or send them to me and I'll take the risks.

Electronic communications are no different from every other

form, and there should be no need for complex guidelines, rules and restrictions. As long as everyone is clear on your company's policy, none of these potential dangers will grow out of hand. People must take personal ownership of their e-mails, even after pressing send.

44 | In need of a rebrand

In the consumer and business world, brands are king. Companies spend millions of pounds every year on the creation, build and protection of what is in effect their main image, and sales weapon. Brands represent everything about a company, by association, and often it is a simple picture, letter or image that conveys a whole set of values, feelings and buying decisions. Scottish Widows, McDonalds and the musical *Les Miserables* are three strong examples.

Companies rated as rising stars for the future are those with very clearly positioned, confident and identifiable brands, which:

- Build customer loyalty.

- Present a feel-good factor.

- Position the whole organization, its activities and goals.

Where do we, as an overall industry, stand in the branding and image stakes? Until recently we had no brand or group identity whatsoever, however that problem was resolved last year. Launched on *News at Ten* to attract maximum publicity, widely splattered (literally) across the national press and billboards, and now available in chocolate form from your local newsagent. Ladies and gentlemen, I present to you, IT – the millennium bug.

A much-needed campaign, brilliantly portraying the dangers ahead through an image that is far from cute and cuddly. The downside of this campaign, however, is that it is the only brand IT has.

Clearly, we need a new identity for the future and a group of industry and marketing experts are proposing to invest in a new brand for IT, to establish a new, positive image. While many IT companies have established strong brands in their own right – Microsoft, IBM and Oracle are all major business players on the world stage – we have no umbrella brand that represents all elements of IT. The proposal is for a new logo that will attract graduates into IT, as well as painting an exciting story based more on the need for interpersonal skills than technology. Marketing experts will be involved, and these independent experts will advise on how IT looks in the eyes of people outside the industry.

It is time to reposition our industry, and through this realize the opportunities for IT in business. Many organizations have done this, for many reasons:

- To achieve goals that have eluded them (e.g. the Labour Party).

- To reposition after poor publicity (e.g. Marks and Spencer).

- To relaunch as a global player (e.g. Axa).

Wires, strange terminology and lines of code have dominated our short history. Let us rally to support this excellent initiative, which has the real opportunity to bury this image forever.

If we are to play our part in shaping the future of UK plc, we need to attract new people, at all levels. Time and again people cite our image as being a major reason for not coming into IT. As we at last cross over the Rubicon that is the year 2000, we have the opportunity to transform IT, shape a new future, and bury the wires and cables forever.

45 | So what?

We all know, but rarely admit, that most IT projects, packages and software fail to deliver real business benefits. IT departments are having to constantly justify their presence as a business asset. Projects that are late, over budget or fail to meet their aims do not help with this justification.

Everyone says there is no such thing as IT work, only business projects. They are right, of course. However, in reality, most business customers still fail to take ownership in this way. Breaking down each and every piece of work by business needs will help everyone to understand, and take on, their responsibilities.

All business applications, packages and software consist of:

- Features;

- Advantages;

- Benefits.

Features

Features are those parts of a system that are never used. Perhaps the needs changed during the project, or additional specifications were added. Features are present in all systems; the problem comes when they dominate. For example, what percentages of PowerPoint or Freelance do most people use in every day work? Probably 20 per cent at most. They do not need to use more, and do not have the time.

And so it is with many in-house systems. A relatively simple business need becomes a complex application, full of functionality that seemed a good idea at the time, but adds nothing to the organization's aims. Indeed, programs are often added later in a project, specifically to bypass code already written. Features add nothing to the bottom line, delay development, and cost more money.

Next time you develop a system, make sure you spot the features, and leave them out.

Advantages

Advantages are the parts of packages and programmed developments that make life easier, are nice to have or used by very few, but cost far more to develop than their results can justify. Advantages are often justified as 'non-tangible'. This is a cop-out, if it can't be measured, don't include it. On a pure cost versus benefit basis, advantages add no bottom-line gain to a company. Advantages are better than features, but not by much.

Benefits

Corporate IT in business must focus on the delivery of tangible, measurable and repeatable benefits. Benefits provide competitive and corporate advantage. They lie at the heart of successful projects.

All projects must be justified on the basis of the benefits they deliver. Forget the never used, or nice to have, we do not have time, resource and energy to waste. Be absolutely ruthless with all proposed projects, and in all reviews you carry out.

Benefits come from on time, or early delivery, so go live with something sooner rather than waiting for the complete picture later. They are measured against initial investment, so focus your spend on the core functionality your company needs.

Most of all, they come from staying ahead of the competition, and to do this every single IT project must put you ahead of your competition. Forget features, be aware of the cost of advantages, and deliver benefits.

46 | Best sourcing

In the early 1990s, partly as a result of so many companies reeling at the disasters caused by downsizing, whole areas of technical support were outsourced. Some high-profile deals were signed for ten years plus. Now many companies are pulling these areas back in house, realizing that in tomorrow's IT world, infrastructure and its associated skills are business critical.

The latest buzz is to outsource applications development, with whole areas of project teams and development being passed over to third parties. This trend will also change in a few years from now.

This push-me pull-you approach is simply not working. It may be good news for the legal departments, it is not good news for IT departments, or the companies that depend on them.

The successful IT department of the future will focus on *best sourcing*. In doing this they will ask three questions, and adopt three roles:

1　What is best for my company? (business broker).

2　Who will bring about the most effective change, fastest? (change enabler).

3　What skills do I need to keep in house, to ensure I can keep control? (human resources).

Business first

It is a well-worn phrase – business is IT, IT is business. Well, let's put that into practice. IT service providers support a wider, more complex area of business than ever before. There are few areas of any organization that are not impacted by technology or information.

The IT director must adopt an independent role, and go for best of breed – and not just ask, 'who shall I outsource to?'. Internal staff, so often not considered, must be in the frame. The answer may well be entering into a supplier partnership, perhaps to allow for growth in demand, or to outsource on a modular basis.

Masters of change

IT leaders must shake off the technology, and adopt a role as masters of change within their organizations. So called business people will scoff at that statement, arguing that the company must set its business goals first, and IT must meet these needs. Those days are fast disappearing, as technology driven change becomes the norm.

Crown jewels

Strategic skills are spread across all areas of IT, to differing depths and amongst different people. It is not unusual to have someone skilled in both support and development.

Skills that are crucial to business advantage should be present in-house. IT departments need to retain control and strategic ownership, even if large areas are outsourced, and cannot do this if all knowledge is passed out.

Traditional methods of sourcing decisions are out of date, and do not meet the needs, challenges and demands of the future.

To survive and thrive, IT departments must drive the future of their organizations. To achieve this, leaders should source on a considered, independent and modular basis that has little to do with the latest trends, and everything to do with best business.

47 | Local power

Why do people become so upset, angry even, when something goes wrong with their PC? Perhaps we should introduce PC rage (PCR, as it would become known) as a concept to define the way some business users talk to your help-desk when their PC so much as hiccups.

These days, whole mainframe systems going down raise little more than an eyebrow. Last week at Victoria station the electronic board announcing departures was completely blank, and a man calmly announced – 'we are unable to display the time, destination or platform of any trains as the computer is not working'. I bet if that man's own, *personal* computer had broken, affecting just him, as opposed to only a few hundred commuters, he would have been much more concerned.

Question one – who does a PC belong to, when it is working? Answer – its user, of course.

Question two – who does a PC belong to, when it is not doing exactly as expected? Answer – the IT department, of course.

PCs are certainly delivering on the personalization of their name, and we can learn valuable lessons in the art of customer service, psychology and service as a result.

- Do PC users know what to do in the event of a problem? They should have an AA/RAC-type card nearby.

- When a call is received, does someone take specific ownership in IT? The help-desk should allocate this to a named individual.

- Do your service specialists introduce themselves to the PC user, and listen to what is wrong, before starting to repair it? Users want to explain what happened, and feel listened to.

- Between calls, is the user left with a card giving the specialist's name? A small business card should be left with the user.

- If the PC has to be removed, is a replacement supplied? Keep a stock for such eventualities.

- At every stage of the process, is the user kept fully informed of what is happening, what will happen next, and the expected outcome? The help-desk can help with this – do this and you are providing an exceptional service that will be remembered.

- Are the user's expectations being measured? If it is likely to take an hour, say three hours, fix it quicker and you will have a delighted user. They will tell up to three people about the exceptional service they have received.

- Are both the technical and personal problems 'fixed?'. Your specialist should only close calls when the PC user is happy everything is working. If not, you will have a disappointed and angry user. They will tell everyone they meet about the appalling service they have received. When a PC goes wrong, no matter how serious or trivial the technical issue, your success will be determined by how well you handle the user, as a person. With PC problems, perception, ownership and communication rule supreme.

48 The Holy Grail

Who do you turn to for technology advice?

You will receive endless sales calls, full of promise and solutions – but with too few guarantees. You will have many experts within your own department – each with their own, often conflicting opinion. You will also attend conferences and hear how everyone else has found the answers – how much is hype? And while it may have worked for them, will it work for you?

Which supplier to believe? Who to listen to? Which conference to attend? For the first time in our history, technology, and its capability, has overtaken the corporate imagination.

There are scores of new technology companies, each developing and offering products that could make a big difference to your business, and enable you to drive your company forward. There are also many white elephants out there.

The challenge lies in marrying the IT department and the right technology. While many companies offer a technical product and solution, they fail to tell a compelling story, or to talk your language, within your context. You need to know the financial, competitive and strategic advantage – hard business and commercial language. Many technologists are simply incapable of speaking in such a way. Other technology companies simply do not know how to gain access to their target market or the route into an IT director. An IT catch-22.

We must bring together IT directors and the solutions they seek. Technology companies must market their products in 'what's in it for the IT department' terms, and the IT director must take steps to search out the products that will drive their department, and company, forward.

- Appoint a futurologist with clear ownership of identifying the technology for you – ensure they consult widely, taking in all opinion. Once a decision is made you must have collective responsibility – or there will be costs, and chaos.

- Consider corporate venturing; share the investment costs in a product in exchange for exclusive use. This way, you would also secure expert advice on how to ensure the new technology delivers.

- When you receive the magic sales call with all the promises you need, ask the supplier to put their money where their mouth is – and guarantee their product or service. If it does not achieve what they say, you will not pay them. That will separate the real from the hype.

- Only attend conferences that confront the realities, and that prompt a debate on issues you can identify with.

It is easy to cite existing, reactive projects and pressures as an excuse for not moving forward. It is often difficult to reconcile so many different options, and opinions. Both of these hurdles must be overcome.

It will be the companies that make time and investment available for such future planning that will have competitive advantage in the future.

With the speed that technology is advancing, the differences between success and failure lies in clear decisions, speed and action.

49 | The hidden costs

Remote working requires IT leaders to strike an elusive balance between trust and control. The advantages of operating from anywhere are many, and many companies have been quick to take advantage of them:

- People can now work according to their lifestyle.

- There are more opportunities relating to maternity leave, and returning to work.

- Many surveys conclude that people are more effective when working from home.

- People can work as they travel, perhaps saving time later.

- Benefits to the environment of less vehicles on the road.

- Less commuters during rush hour periods.

This is not the whole story – there is a downside. Virtual working offers with it many dangers, for staff, their leaders and companies:

- People can become lonely, less motivated and out of touch with corporate developments, and office gossip, so important to the social elements of working.

- Their managers have the difficult task of remote leadership; ensuring communications reach everyone, while ensuring equal treatment to all. For example, such a flexible way of working may not be available to help-desk staff, and they may deem this unfair.

- The risks to the company are enormous, and relate to bottom line costs.

The IT press has recently been full of horror stories about unauthorized internet access, e-mail content and enormous telephone costs. These stories usually have one thing in common – discovery after the event, bringing a large shock to budget holders.

Effective management of remote staff, and their activities, comes down to trust, setting clear guidelines and ensuring that suspected breaking of rules can be policed at source.

- Ensure everyone working away takes ownership of the work they are doing, and fully understands the trust being placed in them by the company.

- Make sure that connections to the internet are closed after each access.

- Encourage people to only dial online outside of peak telephone periods.

- Personal e-mails should not be allowed.

- Disciplinary actions will follow unauthorized access to pornography and other personal interest sites.

- Put in place systems that will allow remote monitoring, and provide information and warnings of potential problems.

Some of this may sound like Big Brother, but trust is a two way process, and too often companies and IT departments have only known about huge costs, after the event.

There is insufficient knowledge and information available through on-site technology, let alone adding the strong incentives for people working at home to do as they please. Clearly there has to be flexibility, and you will know who is most likely to abuse remote working. People who will make such arrangements a success will not complain.

I rarely condone the tight management of people, encouraging as much freedom as possible. Too often, however, people are taking advantage of the opportunities, without accepting the accountability, ownership and responsibilities that come with it.

Such people prove very costly to their companies, having mistaken freedom for licence.

50 | The new IT leader – skill set

Business process reengineering is a fad best forgotten, total quality management is disappearing fast from our agendas, but this thing called leadership looks like sticking around for quite a while.
Over the next three weeks this column will look at three aspects of being an IT leader – in reality.

This week we will look at the powerful influence a leader's character, style and behaviour has on their team. The next column explores the importance of identifying, developing and promoting the next generation of IT directors, and finally we shall identify the five pitfalls of leadership.

People in IT are crying out for guidance, leadership and direction. They are ready and willing to give their best – but unsure what to do, where to go, or whom to trust.

It is not often appreciated the incredible power that one person, or a small group of people can have, inside an organization. They influence the motivation of others, the culture in their team (often clones of themselves), and above all the effectiveness and results of their department.

Have you noticed, for example, that the personality of IT directors has a habit of permeating throughout the department? At one extreme there are those who are dynamic, visible and visionary, on the other, those who are passive, never seen and obsessed with detail.

Clearly there are many shades between, but these fundamental extremes demonstrate the difference between doing a job of management, and being a leader. Leadership is an evolving role, no longer about pioneering, more about the ability and desire to inspire, enable and encourage others to achieve their true potential.

True leaders realize that being stuck in a big office is not the best place to appreciate what is really going on – they ensure their front line are free to make all the decisions they need to make. True leaders are not comfortable being perched on top of a contrived hierarchy – they turn hierarchies upside down, and invest their time in supporting their people. Above all, true leaders do not rely on position or job title. They earn respect on the basis of what they are, the values and behaviour they demonstrate in reality.

Many refer to these new dimensions as personal power – a combination of attitude, belief and behaviour. The acid test of leadership is if you were stripped of your title – the power to punish and reward your people – would you still get results?

Every organization has an enormous, latent force waiting to be released. Management will keep it stifled, leadership will set it free. And when it is free, everything else falls into place, automatically.

I call on all IT leaders everywhere, release the incredible power that exists inside your organizations – by influencing just a handful of people, who will in turn inspire others, you will start a ripple effect that will release the creativity, innovation and potential of millions.

51 | The new IT leader – next generation

As an IT director, future leadership is your responsibility. You owe it to yourself, your team and your company to identify and develop future leaders, in particular ensuring that you have invested in your replacement.

Forget old fashioned succession planning, in which you sit down with your HR director, pen and ruler in hand, and draw straight lines with names on. This is far more fundamental than that. It is the deeply personal action of creating a vision of the future, and making it happen.

Most of us avoid doing this, for understandable reasons:

- We do not know the skills our organization will need in the future. A sound argument for doing nothing – but as most IT directors cannot confidently predict the next three months, let alone years, it must be overcome. In the leadership domain the skills, knowledge and behaviours needed in the future are the same as those true leaders display right now.

- There is no one immediately identifiable for such consideration. This is probably because the subject has taken a back seat in the past. Far from being a reason for inaction, this is a strong argument for fast decisions and investment in key people to rectify the situation.

- The IT director feels threatened by grooming their next in line. This implies that we become more indispensable if there is no one to replace us. Cloud cuckoo land! In today's business world your prospects depend upon how well you leverage the talent energy and creativity of those who work for you. Never forget the grim reaper that sourcing strategy can become!

- The company will recruit externally. All IT departments need new faces. However, this is expensive, uncertain and it takes time. If we fill too many key positions externally, what message is being sent to our own high-flyers?

In reality high quality leadership skills are not widely available. As more companies rely on external recruitment the overall position will worsen. Trained people will simply not be available, and departments will be forced to promote staff who are not ready.

We often bemoan the lack of skills available within our own companies, while slashing costs of training at budget time. Because a company's survival, growth and destiny depends on its people, and particularly on its leaders, we simply must invest in the new generation.

We should scour our departments to identify future leaders at every level. Create a programme for your fast-trackers and make sure they are looked after, so they will stay with you as they continue to grow. By making this investment, you will be doing more to secure the future than anything else you could do.

When you decide to move on you will be judged by the strength of assets you leave behind. What will your legacy be? A successful project, a piece of infrastructure, or a dynamic new leader carrying your flag, ready to take on the world?

How do you want to be remembered?

52 | The new IT leader – pitfalls

What are the biggest obstacles to becoming a true leader? The greatest dangers of derailing those who make it? The highest challenges we must rise to, if we are to be move beyond what we do, and arrive at what we are?

In this last of three columns on leadership, we shall consider the five pitfalls of leadership.

Mistaking position for power

Respect has to be earned, loyalty built. Leaders accept that they work for their people, focusing not on their own achievement, but on the success of others. A leader knows that people working in the front line – on the help desk, for example – make the best day to day decisions, and must be empowered to do so. A leader will never lean on their job title, size of office or position in a hierarchy for authority, or pretend they have access to some greater wisdom not available to others.

Practising communication and not openness

A mistake I have made many times. In their rush to involve others, and become a more communicating department, managers will issue briefings, release documents and shower their teams with e-mails. All in the best possible cause, but in reality overkill. Different people need different information. Leaders will practice a policy of openness – anyone in their department has a right to ask for any information they wish, and unless it is company confidential (in which case they will be told why), it will be received.

Providing answers instead of guidance

We love to show we know the solutions, or the best way to do something. As a result we jump into someone else's problem with our size ten answer. At best it will work, and next time we will be asked to help again, and again.... Leaders take time to understand the issue, then ask questions to draw out the best way forward. They also follow up to enquire if it was successful, and if it was they praise – openly.

Putting popularity before respect

We all like to be liked. With your team, however, it can cause major problems. When you become friends with the team with which you lead, you cross over the barrier of professional objectivity. Leaders earn respect, and do not worry about being liked.

Being visible, but not available

Visibility is key – knowing the names of your staff and making sure that you walk the department every day. That is not enough – people are no longer motivated by your presence alone, you must also be available for them, in their time, and on their terms. Many leaders are now ensuring personal accessibility to all, at set times, in specific ways. Most people will never take you up on the offer, but they will admire, applaud and respect your actions.

The path of true leadership is never easy, but the rewards are amazing.

53 | The five flavours of IT director

IT Directors are never bored. There is more variety, change and uncertainty in the role than in any other. As a result, IT leaders and managers come from many backgrounds, with different styles, attitudes and strengths.

Never one to pigeon-hole, I have nevertheless observed five IT director 'types'. None are necessarily 'better' than others, the style needed being driven by business needs at any given time.

The interim manager (IM)

Your IT director has resigned, and it will take several months to find a replacement. Perhaps the company wants to look at the overall role and its future, or to evaluate the internal staff that, with the right development, could fulfil it. The IM specializes in holding the fort. They oversee day-to-day operations until a long-term plan is in place. Many people are choosing this role, as it offers many challenges, and an opportunity to learn while working in different companies.

Key skill: Fast-track learning.

The cultural transformer (CT)

There first priority is the motivation of staff, the release of human potential, and the destruction of hierarchies. Taken to an extreme, this person will actively encourage chaos, providing it enables people, ideas and action to thrive. The CT is visionary, energetic and visible, and thrives in a post downsizing environment. Be careful though, they will want to change everything they touch.

Key skill: The ability to inspire.

The turnaround king (TK)

The IT department is in trouble. Perhaps key projects are off track, costs are soaring or business perception is low. The TK specializes in repositioning a team or department, and on running IT along true business lines. The role is far from negative – they will often fight off an outsourcing threat, or dramatically improve the business perception of IT.

Key skill: Bags of courage.

The project deliverer (PD)

The PD delivers, time and again. Specializing in the consistent completion of IT projects and major tasks, on time, to budget and meeting business needs. Fast becoming a rare breed, the PD will also put in place a process and approach that will ensure IT projects bring real value to their organization.

Key skill: Persistence to deliver, against all odds.

The master of change (MC)

Many organizations are realizing that they are, first and foremost, IT companies, carrying out business activities on top of a fast, flexible infrastructure on which they are totally reliant. The business is IT, and IT is the business. The MC drives all change within their organization. It is a horizontal role rather than a vertical one, with IT ceasing to exist as a separate entity, and running through all business areas.

Key skill: Business vision.

Although everyone will practice different approaches as the needs demand, people will have a favourite, and dominant style. The ideal, of course, would be to have a mix – with at least one of each in your top team.

54 | Awaken the giants within

Statistics suggest we spend one third of our life asleep, a third at work and a third doing what we choose. Given that startling fact, just image how much happier, content and fulfilled we could all be if we all enjoyed our jobs.

How many people wake up on a work morning and think to themselves, as they leap out of bed 'Great – I am going to work today – I simply love my job, and all of the people I work with'.

Inspiring as the message may be, It is very difficult to *carpe diem* when you are overworked, stressed out and rushing around like a headless chicken fixing other people's problems.

Cliché it may be, but the main reason people do not enjoy their work is because they simply do not identify with their organization, and are out of alignment with its identity, culture or values.

This is a dangerous situation from many perspectives, not least the future of the company itself – there is another way.

When a person's values, beliefs and behaviours are aligned with those of their company, the effects are amazing. By all means put in Investors in People, competency based training and a cultural transformation programme, but to succeed, they need to hit, straight on, the single most important factor in liberating a person's true, and total potential.

That is, people will only give their best if they want to. Pay people what you will, delegate, discipline or direct, a person will only ever perform to their most effective, if they choose to.

When organizations work hard to find out the needs, hopes and fears of their people, and alter their culture around these, they begin to enter the world of absolute peak performance, nothing less. Some examples:

- Flexible hours;

- Opportunities for remote working;

- A dress policy decided by staff, not management;

- Involvement in real decision making;

- Investing pension funds ethically, and publicising such investments to staff;

- Asking people for their ideas, and putting them into action;

- Praising people for doing the right things, as well as for doing things right.

The papers are full of culture, stress and putting our lives in balance – ideas and concepts that would have received scant coverage just a few years ago. Now we must take these ideas a stage further, and place them at the cornerstone of commercial reality. In this regard, IT can be a positive enabler on many fronts.

Just imagine the impact on your bottom line if everyone in your team, department and company felt such a belonging, identity and bonding that they felt they were not working for someone else, but rather for themselves.

This must be the aim of every organization as we move into the new millennium. After all, what is an organization if not its people? These people are the very last of your unique selling propositions, ignore them at your peril.

55 | A waste of valuable time!

IT leaders carry out many time consuming activities that yield little value. I recently carried out an informal survey on which tasks fall into this category. The sample (ten IT directors) was not statistically significant and some responses made tongue firmly in cheek, but there are disturbing messages behind the five most often mentioned. They are, in reverse order of wasted time:

Budgeting

The annual budget round has at times descended into farce, in particular:

- Guessing the cost and benefit of IT/business projects.

- Hiding the cost of training inside other cost codes, as it is the first target for cutback.

- Ensuring that as end of year approaches the budget is spent in full, for fear that coming in under budget will lead to it being reduced the following year.

Tip: Ensure projects are budgeted in business areas, not in IT.

Accessing the right information, at the right time

Executive information systems have a lot to answer for. Often, they have done little more than produce more paper and irrelevant detail. As a result ad hoc reports continue to be programmed, and some companies rely more on self-developed spreadsheets.
Tip: Forget data mining, install an information portal in your company.

Playing e-mail tag, or the cc game

Far from making life easier and more effective, e-mails have over complicated the communications process, and many people now write e-mails when none are needed. Furthermore, there seems to be little evidence of e-mail etiquette, with most hassles and wasted time being caused by aggressive/inaccurate mails. This is made ten times worse by other people being copied on the e-mail, often to make a point, sometimes to simply drop the recipient in it.

Tip: Don't start the cc game, and make all e-mails positive, no matter what the provocation. Count to 100 before replying to a provocative e-mail (if you are really busy ask someone to count for you).

Finding out who owns what

Damning indeed. Who owns what in the complex world of today's medium and large companies seems to be a growing concern. When things go wrong inside their own department, IT directors and senior managers have great difficulty finding out who is accountable.

Tip: For mission critical projects and systems, publish accountability in your service charter. Take public ownership for everything that goes wrong, no matter what.

Attendance at internal meetings

The runaway winner. Few of these seem to follow any formal structure or reach clear action based decisions and results, most are an excuse for politics.

Tip: Set a clear, defined outcome at the start of the meeting – and review if it has been achieved.

Attendance at internal meetings

This list has less to do with time management than sanity preservation. They may all have a part to play in our lives, but we can equally play a part by taking control of each, and the many other low-value tasks not included here.

56 | Board level value

'What has the IT director ever done for us?' shouts the CEO to his board, echoing the Monty Python 'What have the Romans ever done for us?' question. When the list begins, the CEO sidesteps, ignores, or looks the other way – his feelings are all about perception, much more powerful than reality.

When faced with this position, tinkering with the real world will do nothing, one has to go deeper, in order to counter, deflect and dissolve the massive, negative publicity.

Such CEOs are often suffering from spending too long with their heads stuck in sandcastles. After all:

- Who changed the dates?

- Who altered the budgets?

- Who changed their minds after asking for a swing, then a slide, then a roundabout, then a swing that only swings forward, then one for half price, then one in three days time, then?

Time for positive, powerful and proactive action from the IT leader. Time to stand up and be counted, to announce that they and their entire department will, from this moment on, be measured against the return on investment (ROI) they will bring for their company.

The IT priority on the CEO's lips remains financial – Y2K, total cost of ownership, budget expenditure, all combine to support the view that IT is there to take, and not to add. A drain on natural resources.

This has to change – by the IT leaders deciding to measure the real ways they and their department are adding real value to the business, at every level. That they are all, fundamentally, business people. The IT director who is serious about delivering a quantifiable, and measurable ROI must do many things differently:

- Create outstanding measurement/reporting/communicating infrastructures.

- Provide a clear contract (service charter) balancing what a company wants with what a company can afford.

- Put in information systems that track the use of desktops/PCs – and quantify the value they bring.

- Market the IT department through powerful interpersonal relationships, at all levels.

- Quantify the real costs and benefits for all projects.

- Relate everything you do, and plan to do, directly with the company's bottom line.

When the cry goes up, 'down with the Romans/IT department, what have they done for us?', IT leaders must have the allies who immediately leap to their feet and point out, 'what about the aqueducts/inventory systems?'; 'what about the roads/payroll and pensions systems', etc.

Work to put those allies in place, and take ownership of the relationship with your CEO, so that the original question never arises. IT directors who run their departments like a business, delivering on ROI, focus their attention on being a strategic business asset. Achieve this, and it will not be long before the 'allies' are queuing at the gates and then going out into the marketplace to spread the 'word' themselves.

Then the laughter can stop, and IT will be seen as a value, and not simply a cost.

57 | The future is on their side

The marketing, media and PR world seem to have grasped the concept. Most companies, regardless of size, have not. The new technology, information and knowledge experts, are the young. Game companies employ them, parents learn from them, and business pages are full of entrepreneurial stories about them. Traditional business must move fast to catch up.

The irony is that this new opportunity-aware generation do not consider themselves technology geniuses, they have simply opened their minds a bit wider, and embraced the possibilities. Indeed, the very word technology does not enter their minds. And there's the rub, while technophobes react against IT as a confusing and faceless industry, this new breed do not even think about it – it is just another part of life to get on with.

Combine this thought with the apparent national hunt for, and shortage of, non-executive directors, and a winning formula emerges. Take on one of these youngsters as a non-executive director, a boardroom adviser with a two-fold brief:

1 To add their thoughts and expertise to your IT systems.

2 To update the board on how to harness new technologies.

This idea will not be popular with all. Some larger companies are so driven by complex hierarchies, politics and corporate dust they would not know how to cope with, let alone implement, such a suggestion.

IT directors may well find the idea unpalatable, struggling as they are to find a boardroom voice of their own.

To these people I say this. Who are the new entrepreneurs? Who are the people taking ideas and turning them into reality – fast. If they can do it on their own, just imagine what they can do for your organization if given finance, and a free hand.

Forget the traditional business thinking, the future is not what it used to be. IT leaders can take the lead, by finding and recommending the right person to come in at this level. They will then become an independent adviser to the IT department, as well.

What today's young may lack in business savvy they more than make up for in youthful vigour and an extraordinary capacity to learn, investigate and energise.

Where do we find such people? Through the internet, of course. Through business schools and universities, or in one of the many net-based magazines. Just imagine, a small box advert could save you a fortune looking for that elusive non-executive director.

Consider the skills you are looking for in a non-exec. Seeing the future before it happens is likely to rank very high, as is grooming an independent, fresh point of view.

The future of successful enterprise is all about free spirits, about transforming technology, people and communications into opportunities, speed and action.

No longer can wisdom be attributed simply on the basis of age, or experience. These are important attributes and must be valued, but companies that are serious about shaping a compelling destiny will also seek out the young.

58 | Supplier emotion

Evidence strongly suggests that as human beings, emotions play a huge part in our decision-making process. Apply this to IT supplier selection, and we may have the root cause of the crises being faced by so many customers.

Think about it. We put in complex processes to select our partners, issue large invitations to tender that bring even bigger responses. We have initial presentations, followed by shortlists, more meetings and a final decision. Much time, effort and expense, but when the deal is done, how many suppliers have really been selected by the head, and how many by the heart?

Some IT leaders are now recognizing this, and are including 'gut-feel' within their selection criteria. This is to allow for people's inner feelings, thoughts and concerns to be expressed, however it may be that we are allowing our hearts to rule our heads in other categories as well.

Track record/other customers

Looks factual enough but can easily be peppered with opinion and mixed memories. When reviewing existing and previous customers make sure it is you that selects who to speak with. Ask for a full list of customers and select three at random.

Fit for purpose

Clichés like 'exceeding expectations' and 'professional service' must be challenged, and specific details provided. If you are an insurance company, and a supplier promises to focus on improving business performance, ask them precisely how many extra policies will be sold as a result of selecting that supplier.

Quality of tender

Who reads these responses, anyway? Many suppliers who win contracts work hard to make their submissions look and feel the part, when in fact they can be little more than an expensive cover filled with too much general information and promises and too few guarantees. With tenders, customers get what they asked for. My advice is to focus on the three most important priorities, and invite short, succinct and relevant replies. This also has the advantage of ensuring that all suppliers can afford to respond, and not just the big players who are so good at playing the game.

Clearly building strong, trusted relationships is core to future success, and emotions play a huge part in that process, but let's do it at the right levels. In some areas of the public sector we have the ridiculous position of major outsourcers and suppliers cosying up to the government and high-level leaders, while in the real world of delivery things are falling apart all around them. The cost to the taxpayer is huge, to UK plc even greater.

Please do not misunderstand me, as with most things in life, our heart plays an important role in business. On supplier selection, it is perhaps playing too big a role, and having too much influence at the wrong levels. Perception is absolutely crucial, but we must ensure that reality has a say, as well.

59 | Compliant or not?

We're all ready for the year 2000 then, that's all sorted and behind us. Or is it? I hesitate to ask this question, as in the USA; analysts are being placed on blacklists for predicting doom and gloom. Indeed, I had hoped not to revisit this issue, but recent publicity, statistics and statements have caused me some concern, and confusion.

On my left we have the loud company/shareholder assurances from the private sector, confident in their compliance, while on my right we have the most startling information hitting us every single day.

Then we have the government league tables – presumably printed to give the hard working IT departments a motivational boost. And what about the confusing statements from organizations that admit to not being compliant, that they are confident they will have contingency plans in place. For how long can UK plc work in contingency mode?

At the end of 1996 I remember reading that if an organization was not Y2K compliant, it was too late. And yet even today, three years later, there are people who say it is not too late if you start now, and that there are solutions out there that will ensure your compliance. They can't both be right.

A time machine, a time machine, my Action 2000 leaflet for a time machine.

Besides, what does compliance actually mean? I assume it means total and absolute confidence that companies are sure their systems will run correctly into and beyond the year 2000. However, the typical mainframe installation runs millions of lines of code. Across a code-base of this size, remedial work alone won't catch every bug.

The really confident companies have recognized this, and have used date forward aged testing, combined with analysis that provides an exact report of which lines of code have been tested, and will function correctly in post Y2K.

We now have almost three months to the dreaded deadline, and we are faced with the ultimate irony in the precise, specific, logical world of IT – no one knows what will happen.

While it can be tempting to adopt a fix on fail strategy or simply believe the 'we're on course to be compliant' statements, true leadership is required at this late stage.

Proactive action is needed now in order to address this issue before it poses a threat to your corporate existence.

This column always strives to be positive, and I have no wish to be on anyone's blacklist, so I will say this – by committing to thorough testing compliance can still be achieved in the time remaining. I may be wrong, but who knows? Besides, if you are not compliant, what choice do you have? Better than wait and see.

60 | E-government

Dear Alex

Congratulations on your appointment as our first e-envoy, and on the ambitious set of goals you and Patricia Hewitt have set.

The overall aim to make UK the best environment in the world for e-commerce is hugely exciting, much needed, and with the talent we have in this country, eminently achievable. Given the track record of progress by committee, however, it is also wildly ambitious. Government (of all flavours) is more renowned for its lengthy research, long reports and political blocking than for fast decisions, risk taking and inspirational action.

To achieve the goals you have set, this mould will have to be broken, and quickly. If it is not, government involvement could be the death of the entrepreneurial spirit on which the future success of e-commerce so deeply depends. The rest of the world won't stand by and wait.

Many do not realize the impact that e-commerce will have. Any company acting as a middleman is under direct and immediate threat. Travel agents, estate agents, department stores, publishing, advertising and many others. Right now small groups of people are plotting transaction systems that will change the face of business, forever, and they are not going to wait for government permission, or guidance.

Technology has truly caught up with imagination, and while e-commerce represents the best opportunity for small and medium companies to grow and take market share, it is the biggest threat ever to be faced by large organizations, many of whom have a rudder no bigger than that of the *Titanic*. I know several of these who are starting to turn, utilizing their vast resources and intellectual capital in new directions. Equally, I know many that are doing too little, too late.

To achieve the outcomes and success needed, we must pool together the skills, experience and resources at our disposal like never before:

- IT directors must be involved at an early stage – please do not fall into the traditional government trap of only consulting with suppliers.

- We must remove all barriers and red tape that stifle e-commerce initiatives and transactions.

- E-commerce should be the catalyst to draw in a whole new generation of computer users, and IT awareness.

- Government must invest in public sector e-commerce (an area sorely neglected to date), and streamline communication and information around Westminster.

- Involve more entrepreneurs than civil servants.

- Ensure at least one person on the Information Age Management Board is aged below 20.

We have in the United Kingdom some of the most intelligent, insightful and inspiring business and IT leaders in the world. Many are already playing a large part in e-commerce. Just imagine the powerful and positive impact on UK plc when these forces are focused not just on predicting the future, but working together to shape it.

I support your aims with a passion. Provided you have the authority, are prepared to take action, and to move very quickly, you will be successful.

61 | Don't dispute – learn to dance

There is so much worry, fear and negativity surrounding customer/supplier relationships, that developing them into trusted partnerships becomes ever more difficult. At best, we tolerate each other, engaging in ongoing pleasantries as we go about our business, interspersed with warning shots across the bow – about cost, service or anything else we can think of. At worst, we are simply expecting things to go wrong, and, with weighty contracts at the ready, ready to pounce.

What an opportunity we are missing – to forge powerful strategic alliances with our suppliers. Alliances that will enable real competitive advantage for both parties, that will help us with our decision making and cross skilling, and that will add real value to both parties.

A supplier/customer relationship is not determined during the selection and negotiation/contract phase, nor when events take a turn for the worse, but during the ongoing, mundane relationships in between. And at all levels, the success of the relationship is as much dependent on communication at the coalface as it is on your relationship with the supplier's representative or leader.

It is in this very area – during the ongoing work – that most benefits can be gained. As an IT director ask yourself:

● When did you last involve a supplier in a strategic decision for your department?

● When did you and your supplier last second staff – one to the other?

- Market awareness is very important to you – when did you last seek the opinion of your supplier in an industry or business sector issue?

- When did you last thank your supplier for good work – or pay their invoice early?

These actions go way beyond gestures, and open up a new spirit of cooperation and care in the relationship. They demonstrate a mutual determination to build a long-term alliance for the future. Aside from the questions above – there are immediate ways a supplier can help their customer:

- Advise on how your IT service compares with others – suppliers do not need to give names or betray confidences from other customers – general advice can help enormously.

- Host a drinks/buffet event for your IT director's business customers – you gain some publicity, help the IT director and department 'sell' themselves in a better light than when things are going wrong, and you have an opportunity to convey a key message to business decision makers.

- Ensure that your customers' culture and code of conduct (written or observed) are embedded in each and every one of your people.

- Work hard to cooperate with other suppliers in the organization.

- Never, ever, run down your client organization – to anyone.

Here, on our very doorstep, we have access to the outer world through companies we work with every single day.

There is so much doom and gloom about customer/supplier relationships. Take a strong decision to put the negatives to one side, and focus on some positive actions that will take your relationship forward to new strengths, heights and achievements.

62 | Sorry has to be the hardest word

When we were younger, our parents taught us that it was good manners to say 'sorry', and when we should say it. What we didn't learn until we became IT leaders, is how often we were expected to use the word. 'Sorry' seems to have become the main word used by IT departments to their business customers. The system goes down, a project is late, or a PC fails to arrive on time – 'sorry'.

Very different from a few years ago, when we would dive under our desks when things went wrong – hoping the problems would go away. Then account management came along, and IT departments became more 'customer focused' overnight. All of these people who had previously been taught to hide at the first sign of trouble, were now expected to become ambassadors for the IT department.

Central to this role was the ability to sprint. The moment disaster strikes, account managers led the charge into the business areas, with the latest news of what had happened, when it would be fixed, and ready to say 'sorry'.

Excellent, you might well say. At last IT was moving from its faceless ivory tower to becoming far more visible, and aware.

Fine in principle, however this approach has a gaping flaw, perception. When we only communicate with our customers in the event of things going wrong, the very sight of someone from IT approaching becomes enough in itself to cause sweat, fear and panic.

Oh no, it is someone from IT, they are approaching me very fast and they look extremely apologetic, it must be *bad news*. And the reverse starts to happen, whereas before it was IT people who took cover in the event of a problem, now it is their business customers who do the same, for fear of hearing news they just do not want to hear. It can very quickly become self-fulfilling.

Such negative associations, in whatever extreme, are very damaging, but can easily be turned to our advantage, and dramatically improve the perception of the IT department. You and I know that for the vast majority of the time, events go well for IT in business – and these are the times to be proud of, to go onto the front foot, and to be seen to be adding real benefit.

Perception is very often seen as reality, so let's ensure we take command of it:

- That we are visible when all is well.

- We are proud of our many achievements.

- Ownership of events, and projects, does not just lie with IT.

- We go on the front foot in driving the business forward in a positive way.

How we are seen to be doing plays a huge part in people's perceptions of IT. The power players in our organizations will make up their minds about us on the basis of their beliefs, and it is these we must focus on, influence and control.

63 | **Foundations for the future**

IT certainly sets the trend for where business will be in the future. With the right investment, expertise and action, electronic commerce, CRM (customer relationship management) and all the other exciting in-phrases will drive our organizations forward, and leave our competitors behind.

All of this makes IT an incredibly exciting area to work. Probably the biggest forward change driver in any business, our agenda as we move across into 2000 looks very positive, and powerful.

I can remember just a few years ago when the focus was very different. Our business peers would judge us on project success or failure, on how much technology was really costing (total cost of ownership) and on how we aligned ourselves with business people, agendas and goals. Internally we would be grappling with low morale and skill shortages, supplier disputes and fallouts, and the eternal catch 22 of trying to provide everything our organizations needed, at the price it was prepared to pay.

For so many columns, conferences and conversations to focus on the new, exciting agenda, is a major leap forward for all of us. Clearly we have at last come to terms with the challenges of the past. Or are we just ignoring them, hoping they have gone away?

We should applaud the new, positive agenda, which will place IT at the heart of an organization. However, we must also make sure that our foundations are not ignored, and keep some sense of reality among all of the hype.

- Eight out of ten IT business projects fail to meet their targets, four out of ten collapse completely.

- The real cost of PCs is growing, as business usage soars.

- Most CEOs in the world still feel that IT is out of touch with their organizations.

- Many infrastructures are too brittle.

- Some skill shortages continue. Staff turnover (at all levels) will soar post-millennium.

- There are more supplier disputes reaching court today than ever before.

This column always aims to be positive, but it must also have its finger on the pulse of the world of the IT leader, and on corporate IT in business.

My fear is that unless some of these long-term challenges are resolved, once and for all, our foundations for other strategies will be unsound. Clearly we must move forward at the same time, and this dilemma is not an easy one to resolve.

- Many of the new tools and technologies can be used to address existing problems.

- Each and every one of these seemingly impossible problems can, and must, be resolved.

- We should share all the issues we are facing with our business peers.

Many of the latest IT developments will transform organizations forever. It is up to all of us to ensure this transformation is constructed on something more solid than sand.

65 | One voice, one power

Consultants make a shed load of money out of this thing called business alignment – but what does it mean, and how can it be achieved? Alignment means ensuring that IT services are closely matched with business aims, culture and performance. Easy to talk about in theory, difficult to achieve in practice.

Most often, business and IT strategies are rarely matched to ensure the same approach, goals and vision. As a result, business plans often leave IT behind, the result being a low perception of IT and the support they provide. On the other hand, IT may be setting the pace, and be pioneering new and leading edge technologies for which the business itself is simply not ready. This will cause as many problems, at every level.

The most effective method of achieving total balance, a one-world vision, is to wrap the IT strategy around that of the organization as a whole, and vice versa. The corporate strategy will be put in place, with full involvement from the IT director. The IT strategy will then be developed to reflect this business vision in some areas, and to drive it forward in others. Both plans will then be mapped onto each other, section by section.

The final document will be a combination of what the business wishes to achieve, and how it will do so. Each goal, project and activity will be followed by the relevant IT delivery plan. Equally, each and every IT project will be followed by a section providing the clear business aims, resources and benefits.

Organizations that have mastered this dual approach achieve stunning improvements in all aspects of their use of IT, and its effectiveness in driving their business forward. In addition to improved planning, and understanding by all involved in the vision and journey, such contentious issues as ownership, prioritization and delivery can be more fully explored, and explained.

The approach can be extended to other activities within an organization, such as budget planning, training and recruitment. As it develops, the areas previously known as 'IT' and 'business' will begin to merge, with leaders throughout having a wider understanding of the big picture, and how it will be achieved.

Adopting this method also leads to improved measurement of IT value. It will only be possible to list each and every IT activity as it is matched to a business justification, rather than being done for its own sake.

When reasons for IT spend are explained in such hard commercial language, the perception in, and influence of, the IT department will rise. Budget negotiations will also become easier, as they begin to take place in business language.

Everyone talks about IT being core to business activities, but it is all too rare in reality. By adopting this approach, and involving a wide range of leaders in its development and operation, the organization will truly go forward with one vision, one voice, and as an awesome force of strategic power.

Appendix | Contents – sorted by category

Category	Chapter No	Title	Date published
	57	The future is on their side	2 September 1999
	4	Beware of suspect packages	6 August 1998
	8	A date too far?	3 September 1998
	20	Promises promises	26 November 1999
	32	Linux leaves school	11 March 1999
	35	Bargain basement	1 April 1999
	48	The Holy Grail	1 July 1999
Supplier/business partnerships	58	Supplier emotion	9 September 1999
	61	Don't dispute – learn to dance	30 September 1999
	1	Beyond belief	16 July 1998
	7	Emotions must give way to reason	27 August 1998
	12	Supplier fallout	1 October 1999
	19	A wolf in sheep's clothing	19 November 1999
	39	Twenty-first century partnerships	29 April 1999
	42	Avoiding the fault line	20 May 1999
The future	2	What happens after what comes next?	23 July 1998
	14	IT directors planning for recession	15 October 1999
	24	A full twelve months	14 January 1999
	33	Future shock	18 March 1999
	63	Foundations for the future	14 October 1999
Total cost of ownership	21	Raising the standard	3 December 1999

Category	Chapter No	Title	Date published
	22	Volume over value	10 December 1999
	37	Chaos or freedom?	15 April 1999
	49	Hidden costs	8 July 1999
Y2K	11	Shall we dance?	24 September 1998
	27	League table 2000!	4 February 1999
	59	Compliant or not?	16 September 1999

Index